F1868.2 .S47 2004

Sheehan, Sean, 1951-

Jamaica /

2004.

2007 05 04

HUMBER COLLEGE
LAKESHORE CAMPUS
LEARNING RESOURCE CENTRE
3199 LAKESHORE BLVD. WEST
TORONTO, ONTARIO M8V 1K8

DISCARD

W9-BDA-947
0 1341 0963225 4

CULTURES OF THE WORLD®

JAMAICA

Sean Sheehan & Angela Black

BENCHMARK BOOKS

MARSHALL CAVENDISH
NEW YORK

Humber College Library

PICTURE CREDITS
Cover photo: © Melanie Acevedo/Getty Images
APA: 23, 27, 28, 29, 36, 61, 62, 80, 82, 85, 88, 104, 116 • Art Directors & TRIP: 1, 6, 20, 42,
55, 66, 95, 130 • Eye Ubiquitous: 8, 40 • Anne Bolt: 6, 37, 40, 87, 100, 103, 112, 119, 121,
124, 125 • Susanna Burton: 73, 91 • Camerapress: 60, 79, 96 • Focus Team: 47, 52, 54, 80,
94, 112, 120 • Hulton-Deustch: 24, 30, 86, 108, 109, 114 • Hutchison Library: 3, 20, 64, 66,
69, 75, 89, 92, 95, 120, 123 • Image Bank: 4, 9, 17, 19, 44, 56, 57, 65, 72, 76, 105, 117, 129
• B. Klingwall: 12, 16, 18, 22, 26, 32, 33, 38, 42, 71, 74, 81, 83, 128 • Jason Laure': 51, 104,
131 • Life File: 5, 11, 13, 21, 25, 43, 47, 78, 93, 94, 102, 122 • Lonely Planet Images: 32
• Photobank International: 48, 56, 127, 131 • Reuters: 35 • K. Seah: 15 • David Simson:
3, 30, 72, 88 • R. Vargliese. 115   EMI Records. 97 (Picture of Jimmy Cliff reproduced
with permission from EMI Records)

ACKNOWLEDGMENTS
Thanks to Deborah A. Thomas, Assistant Professor, Department of Cultural Anthropology
at Duke University, for her expert reading of this manuscript.

PRECEDING PAGE
Two Jamaican girls sport hairstyles typical of their culture, including a specially braided
version of the dreadlocks of the nation's Rastafarian tradition.

Marshall Cavendish Benchmark
99 White Plains Road
Tarrytown, NY 10591
Website: www.marshallcavendish.us

© Times Media Private Limited 1996, 1994
© Marshall Cavendish International (Asia) Private Limited 2004
All rights reserved. First edition 1994. Second edition 2004.

® "Cultures of the World" is a registered trademark of Marshall Cavendish Corporation.

Originated and designed by Times Books International
An imprint of Marshall Cavendish International (Asia) Private Limited
A member of Times Publishing Limited

All rights reserved. No part of this book may be reproduced or utilized in any form or
by any means electronic or mechanical, including photocopying, recording, or by an
information storage and retrieval system, without permission from the copyright owner.

Library of Congress Cataloging-in-Publication Data
Sheehan, Sean, 1951-
Jamaica / by Sean Sheehan. — 2nd ed.
    p. cm. — (Cultures of the world)
Includes bibliographical references and index.
    ISBN 0-7614-1785-0
1. Jamaica—Juvenile literature. I. Title. II. Series: Cultures of the world (2nd ed.)
F1868.2.S47 2004
972.92—dc22   2004007676

Printed in China

765432

CONTENTS

Jamaica's wide variety of fruit and vegetables adds to its rich food heritage.

Colorful wooden fish models at a handicraft market in Ocho Rios.

INTRODUCTION

THE THIRD LARGEST ISLAND in the Greater Antilles of the West Indies is known as a tropical paradise. Jamaica has some lush foliage and exotic wildlife, and its waters are clear and skies blue for most of the year. However, the island has suffered environmental damage due to industry and natural disasters.

Most Jamaicans are descendants of African slaves who were brought to the island by the Spanish and English between 1513 and 1834 to work on sugar plantations. When slavery was abolished in 1838, people from Asia, Europe, and the Middle East came to the island to work on plantations.

Decades of intermarriage between immigrants and Jamaicans have produced the unique ethnic diversity that characterizes modern-day Jamaican society. The national motto—out of many, one people—describes how a small nation of disparate peoples blended together to create a rich cultural heritage.

GEOGRAPHY

LOCATED 480 MILES (772.5 km) south from the Florida coast, the Caribbean island of Jamaica is slightly smaller than the U.S. state of Connecticut. Stretching 146 miles (235 km) from east to west and, at its widest, 50 miles (80 km) from north to south, Jamaica has a land area of nearly 4,182 square miles (10,831 square km), some 80 percent of which is mountainous.

Set in the Caribbean Sea, Jamaica and the other islands of the West Indies owe their existence to prehistoric volcanic activity in the region. Millions of years later, earthquakes continue to threaten the islands. Jamaica's capital city, Kingston, was twice destroyed by earthquakes in recent times—once in 1692 and again in 1907.

ONCE UPON A TIME

Approximately 70 million years ago, a cataclysmic upheaval deep in the earth's crust forced up the immense mountain range that is today the backbone of Mexico and Central America. One branch of this range extended east toward the present-day location of Jamaica. Most of the extension was submerged under water, but the higher peaks remained above sea level. These peaks included the Blue Mountains that today dominate the eastern section of the island of Jamaica.

The ancient volcanic activity in the region also folded the terrain in some places and raised seabeds. The elevated seabeds became a vast cemetery of marine life forms. Over millions of years, the skeletons of minute organisms formed a layer of limestone.

Subsequent tectonic movements, about 20 million years ago, pushed the limestone cap out of the water. The topography of Jamaican land, about half of which rises 1,000 feet (305 m) above sea level, is the result of these prehistoric seismic events.

We mus' tell map
We don't like we position,
Please kindly take we out o' sea
And draw we in de Ocean.

—from a poem by Jamaican poet and activist Louise Bennett

Opposite: **The Blue Mountains abound with ferns and flowers.**

7

A rainbow over the Blue Mountains, whose north-eastern slopes receive the most rain on the island and are thus a major source of water for rural and urban communities.

THREE REGIONS

Jamaica can be divided into three main geographical regions: eastern highlands, central highlands, and coastal lowlands.

EASTERN HIGHLANDS   Covering about 20 percent of Jamaica, the eastern highlands rise to more than 5,000 feet (1,500 m), reaching their highest point, 7,402 feet (2,255 m), at Blue Mountain Peak. The Blue Mountains dominate the eastern parishes of Saint Thomas, Portland, and Saint Andrew.

Other mountain ranges in eastern Jamaica include the John Crow Mountains in the extreme east, and the Port Royal range that provides a scenic background to the capital, Kingston.

The Blue Mountains, which bisect the eastern highlands on an east-west axis, form a watershed for more than 120 rivers. The rivers flow so steeply down the mountains that few are navigable. Two of the more well-known rivers in the region are the Rio Grande and the Yallahs.

CENTRAL HIGHLANDS Karst scenery characterizes central Jamaica. The karst landscape is the result of erosion. Rainwater erodes limestone surfaces in the central region, forming unique geographical features such as sinkholes, irregular landscapes, and underground streams.

Small round hills and large sinkholes, or cockpits, dominate the limestone plateau of Cockpit Country. The hills and hollows make the region unsuitable for habitation or agriculture. In fact, in the 17th and 18th centuries, the region's inaccessibility made it a good hiding place for Maroons—freed or runaway slaves.

The paths of rivers in karst country are particularly fascinating. Hector's River, for example, starts in the central plateau and flows west for 12 miles (19 km) before disappearing into a sinkhole. It resurfaces in the south as One Eye River, sinks again, and reappears in the west to form the headwaters of Black River.

The river basins of the region also provide valuable agricultural land, such as Queen of Spain's Valley in the northwest, Nassau Valley south of Cockpit Country, and Saint Thomas-in-the-Vale in the east.

Bamboo rafts, once used to transport bananas from the interior to towns and ports, now take tourists upriver to enjoy the lush rainforest.

COASTAL LOWLANDS Jamaica's plains are narrow in the north and broader in the south. The most extensive lowland region stretches from Liguanea Plain near Kingston west to about the midpoint of southern Jamaica. The most important farming areas are in Savanna la Mar in the parish of Westmoreland and the western Black River Valley in the parish of Saint Elizabeth.

Hurricane Gilbert, one of the most ferocious storms ever recorded in the western hemisphere, struck Jamaica in September 1988. More than 30 Jamaicans died in the storm, and about 20 percent of the island's population lost their homes.

CLIMATE

As on other Caribbean islands, temperatures in Jamaica do not vary significantly during the year and rarely fall below 60°F (16°C). The day range is 75 to 85°F (24 to 29°C), while at night the temperature hovers around 65°F (18°C).

Altitude affects temperature in Jamaica. The general rule is a fall in temperature of 1°F (0.56°C) with every rise in altitude of 300 feet (90 m). This partly explains why the more exclusive suburbs of Kingston, the capital, are located in the foothills, where the weather is cooler than on the plains. Light frost occasionally occurs in winter at the highest points on the island, the summits of the Blue Mountains.

The island receives sudden, heavy downpours during the rainy seasons, which extend from May to June and from September to November. Two weather phenomena affect rainfall in Jamaica: trade winds and hurricanes.

TRADE WINDS Trade winds in the northern hemisphere blow from a high-pressure zone southwest toward the equator, where they are deflected westward by the earth's rotation.

When the winds reach the Blue Mountains, they are forced to rise sharply. As they ascend, they cool considerably and condense to form clouds, which eventually fall as rain. The windward side of the range receives most of the rain. The leeward side of the mountains remains relatively dry, because little moisture is left by the time the winds reach the leeward side. Thus, Port Antonio, located in the northeast, receives about 130 inches (330 cm) of rain annually, and Kingston, located in the southeast, receives only about 30 inches (75 cm). The mountains receive about 200 inches (500 cm) of rain annually.

HURRICANES The months of July through November are hurricane season in Jamaica. The sky darkens and low clouds appear before a hurricane. Then violent winds bring heavy rains and high waves. The winds subside momentarily as the eye of the storm passes, then resume until the storm moves on.

Hurricanes usually hit the eastern end of Jamaica and then move northward. In 1980 Hurricane Allen whipped up towering waves that killed a few people and severely damaged coral reefs on the island's northern coast, such as at Discovery Bay.

While Allen passed near Jamaica's coast, in 1988 Gilbert tore right through the island with windspeeds of more than 100 miles per hour. Besides further damaging coral reefs, which were still recovering from Allen's attack, Gilbert killed more than 20 people on the island and destroyed buildings and crops. Kingston suffered the greatest damage. Having dealt its first blow to Jamaica, Gilbert hit the Cayman Islands and the Yucatan Peninsula even more furiously, earning a reputation as one of the 20th century's most devastating hurricanes.

High winds and waves are common in the hurricane season.

Crocodiles are generally found in or near rivers and swamps, where there is an abundance of food.

FLORA

Little remains of the woodland forest that once covered most of Jamaica. In the southern coastal regions, however, mangrove swamps continue to flourish, because there is no economic incentive to cut them down. Mangroves cope with the salt content of the muddy coastal waters in a variety of ways. Some species have root systems that filter out the salt; others take in the salt and expel it through the leaves or shed leaves that become saturated with salt.

In the west and southwest of the island, there are level areas of grassland with scattered scrub trees. This is known as savanna country, and the land here is not suitable for agriculture.

The ceiba tree, or silk cotton tree, grows to 130 feet (40 m) in height and 50 feet (15 m) in circumference. The name of Kingston's Half Way Tree Road recalls a time when a ceiba tree served as a resting place for women traveling to the capital with their produce. The ceiba tree is not planted for commercial use, although the seeds' fluffy covering was once used to fill life jackets and pillows.

Jamaica has more than 3,000 species of flowering plants, including 200 kinds of orchids. Fern Gully, a 4-mile (6.4-km) road running south of Ocho Rios, boasts more than 500 species of ferns. The blossom of the *lignum vitae*, or wood of life, is the national flower. It is purple, with bright yellow stamens. The plant was once highly valued for its medicinal properties.

Jamaican plants that are cultivated for commercial use include coffee, banana, cacao, yam, okra, ginger, allspice, and sugarcane. Oranges, grapes, melons, and coconuts are common in Jamaica. Other noteworthy plants and trees of the island include breadfruit, mango, pawpaw, guava, and starfruit.

Thick mangrove swamp along Black River in the parish of Saint Elizabeth.

FAUNA

Jamaica's indigenous land animals, such as the manatee and American crocodile, are becoming increasingly rare. Far more common is the mongoose, a ferret-like carnivore that was brought from India to kill rats and snakes on sugarcane plantations.

Jamaican bird life is impressive. There are around 200 bird species, including 25 that are endemic, such as the Jamaican owl. Parrots and hummingbirds are common though no less attractive to birdwatchers. Jamaica is also home to 14 of the world's more than 1,000 species of fireflies. Each species has its own light system that differs from others in color, intensity, and interval between flashes.

13

JAMAICAN BIRDS AND JAMES BOND

The birds of Jamaica are divided into two groups: migratory and indigenous. While the indigenous birds are found in Jamaica all year, the migratory species make the island their temporary home twice a year. In the fall, birds fly south from North America to Brazil's grasslands and Argentina's La Plata marshes, a journey nearly 7,000 miles (11,300 km) long.

When they reach Florida and the Gulf states, the birds cross the Gulf of Mexico and fly over Cuba and Jamaica. About a third of the 60 species of birds that follow this migration route stay in Jamaica through winter. In spring, they fly north by the same route.

One of Jamaica's 25 indigenous bird species is the national bird, the streamer-tailed hummingbird (*left*), better known as the doctor bird, perhaps because of its split tail, resembling a stethoscope, and its black head, which recalls the black top hats doctors once wore. The streamer-tailed hummingbird is depicted in the Air Jamaica logo and on Jamaican currency.

Another bird that has a Jamaican nickname is the John Crow. It has a black plumage tinged with brown, and its feet, naked head, and neck are purplish red. It looks a little like a turkey. John Crows are scavengers. They can often be seen looking for food in garbage dumps. The albino John Crow, called the John Crow Headman, is rarely seen.

Ian Fleming, the writer who created the character of secret agent James Bond, lived in Jamaica for many years, and the Bond movie *Live and Let Die* was filmed in Jamaica. Fleming wrote all his Bond novels on the island and named his hero, James Bond, after the author of one of his favorite books, *Birds of the West Indies*.

LIFE IN THE WATER

The waters around the island of Jamaica are extremely clear, and sunlight penetrates to a depth of 80 feet (24 m). Yellow clumps of seaweed called sargassum drift on the surface of the water. The sargassum is home to a multitude of tiny fish and shrimp, which are eaten by larger fish.

Jamaica's coastal waters brim with reef life (*right*), especially in the north. The reefs contain many species of Caribbean coral. Coral polyps are colorful animals with tube-shaped bodies and tentacles. Some species float in the water, displaying their colorful bodies, while other species live inside skeletons that are formed out of limestone in seawater. They may join to form reefs where the water is shallow, clear, and warm. There must also be currents to wash the corals with oxygen- and nutrient-rich water from the sea.

Reef communities contain an astounding variety of plants and animals. Tropical fish and lobsters inhabiting the numerous crevices

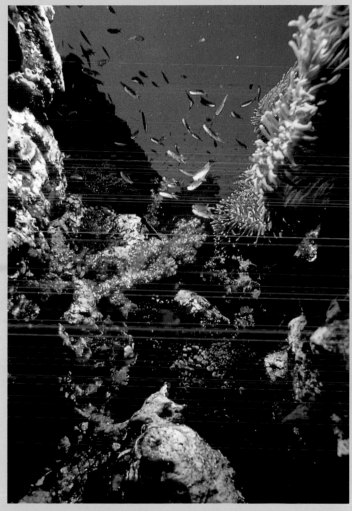

in the reefs attract sharks and barracudas. Parrotfish swallow tiny pieces of coral rock, which contains calcium, to digest the microscopic plants that cling to the rock. At night, the parrotfish wraps itself in a mucous cocoon that protects it from predators.

The Portuguese man-of-war resembles a large jellyfish but is actually a colony of organisms, each with a specialized function. One part of the colony secretes a gas in an organ known as the float, which allows the colony to drift on the surface of the water with the current. Other members of the colony produce tentacles that trail in the water and kill fish on contact. A diver or swimmer who accidentally touches one of these tentacles gets a shocking sting.

The Port Royal mountain range provides a scenic backdrop for Kingston, the capital of Jamaica.

JAMAICAN TOWNS

Urbanization in Jamaica is concentrated in the coastal areas, where the fertile and more level land supports commercial crop cultivation. Most of the island's popular tourist towns—Negril, Montego Bay, Ocho Rios, and Port Antonio—are located along the northern coast, where miles of white sandy beaches attract tourists.

Jamaica's main roads follow the coastline, except in the south where they run farther inland. Only two major roads run in a north-south direction, connecting the central towns.

KINGSTON The seat of government moved from Spanish Town to Kingston in 1872. Kingston is located on the southeastern coast of the island. It has a population of more than half a million and the largest number of English speakers south of Miami, Florida. Kingston occupies more than 10 square miles (26 square km) and is the commercial and cultural nucleus of Jamaica.

Kingston was born out of disaster. It had to be completely rebuilt in 1907 after an earthquake and fires reduced the city to rubble and ash. Today, Kingston is a picturesque city with a mountain range in the background and the seventh largest natural harbor in the world as its waterfront. The University of the West Indies, founded in 1948, sits on land that once belonged to the Hope sugar estate and houses a 17th-century aqueduct. Since the 1970s an area called New Kingston has developed to become the financial center of the capital.

PORT ANTONIO Located on the northeastern coast of Jamaica, Port Antonio overlooks twin harbors East and West. The port prospered at the peak of the banana trade in the early 1900s, but hurricanes and the Panama Disease smothered the trade in the 1930s. Nevertheless, the banana trade jump-started tourism in Jamaica, and Port Antonio had the island's first hotel, Titchfield, which later became a secondary school. Tourism has become the city's main industry.

Picturesque Port Antonio and its twin harbors. In the lower right corner is Navy Island, which once belonged to Hollywood actor Errol Flynn.

Doctor's Cave Beach in Montego Bay is famous for its beautiful beaches and therapeutic spring-water. Jamaica's northern coast is called the Gold Coast for its golden sands and thriving tourism.

MONTEGO BAY Jamaica's second-largest city and its foremost tourist resort ranks as one of the best-known vacation destinations in the Caribbean. Montego Bay is characterized by a string of luxury beach hotels, designer boutiques, and guarded private homes, an extreme contrast to the slums fringing most towns in Jamaica.

Christopher Columbus called the bay by a different name—El Golfo de Buen Tiempo, or Fair Weather Gulf. There are two possible origins of the name Montego: the name of an early colonizer, Montego de Salamanca; or the word *manteca* (man-TAY-kah), meaning fat or lard, a by-product of the wild hogs that once roamed the region.

Montego Bay has several historic sites, including Saint James Parish Church, Sam Sharpe Square, and Rose Hall.

NEGRIL Called Negrillo by the Spaniards, Negril was a shelter for pirates in the 18th century. Until about 20 years ago, it was an isolated fishing village with no telephones or electricity. Then word of its unspoiled beauty spread, and Negril became a popular tourist destination.

The famous Dunn's River Falls near Ocho Rios.

The city's 7-mile (11-km) white-and-aquamarine shore is its most popular attraction. Also of interest is a wetland national park and a 100-foot (30-m) lighthouse that was in service for more than 100 years.

PORT ROYAL Located at the tip of a long, narrow peninsula south of Kingston, the historic town of Port Royal was Jamaica's first trading city. This former naval base was converted to an air base, and today the peninsula is the site of the Norman Manley International Airport. Large-scale restoration, including archeological exploration, is in progress to make Port Royal an important historical destination.

OCHO RIOS The name of Ocho Rios, or Eight Rivers, is erroneously thought to be a Spanish invention. The Spaniards named the city Las Chorreras, or The Waterfalls, after the Dunn's River Falls, not far west of Ocho Rios. The city is a scenic swimming destination popular among Jamaicans and tourists alike. One of Jamaica's largest bauxite mines is located near Ocho Rios.

HISTORY

ANTHROPOLOGISTS BELIEVE that the earliest inhabitants of Jamaica were cave-dwelling Ciboney Indians, who migrated south from what is now Florida around 500 B.C.

Between A.D. 600 and 700, Taino Arawak traveled north from what is now Venezuela and settled on the island now known as Jamaica. They lived in peace, hunting, fishing, and farming, until the Spaniards arrived in 1494. Contact with the foreigners exposed the Taino Arawak to new diseases for which they had no immunity.

Opposite: **Fort Charles is the oldest structure in Port Royal. It was built by the British soon after their conquest of the island in 1655.**

Below: **A 1778 map of Jamaica.**

Bonne: Map of the Island of Jamaica 1778

A replica of a Taino Arawak hut in the National Museum.

THE TAINO ARAWAK

Driven by invading groups, from their homelands in what are today Venezuela and the Guyanas, the Taino Arawak headed north and eventually settled in the Caribbean islands. The Taino Arawak were a seafaring people who lived near the coasts and rivers. At first, the Spaniards, thinking they had sailed half-way around the world and reached India, viewed the Taino Arawak as Indians.

Taino Arawak cave paintings and other archeological finds make it clear that the Taino Arawak were skilled in making tools and everyday implements. One of their inventions—a bed of cotton hung by cords at each end—made a deep impression on the Spaniards, who brought the hammock back to Europe.

Between 60,000 and 100,000 Taino Arawak were living in Jamaica when the Spaniards arrived. They had their own power structure that worked through a system of chiefs and sub-chiefs. Their skill in sailing allowed them to barter with neighboring islanders.

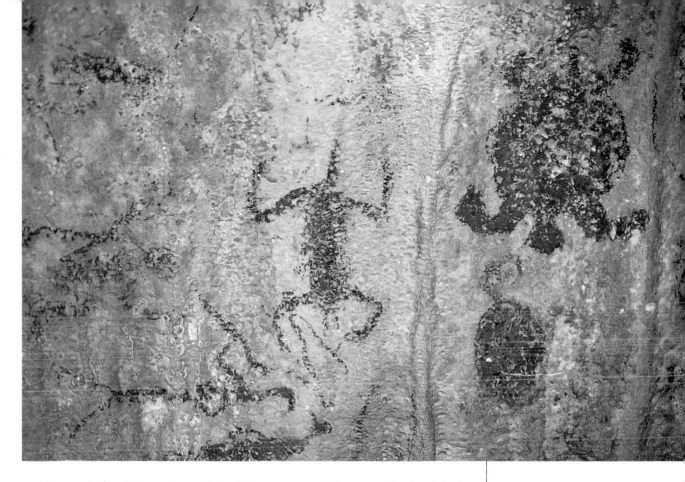

An Arawak painting on a cave wall.

None of the Taino Arawak's skills prepared them to deal with the Spanish invaders, who imposed their own laws and religious beliefs on Taino Arawak society. The Spaniards enslaved the Taino Arawak and, within a relatively short time, the indigenous population of Jamaica dwindled to a tiny minority.

Many of the Taino Arawak in Jamaica died from being overworked. Probably many more died at sea after leaving the island in canoes in an attempt to escape from the Europeans.

Another cause of the decline and eventual demise of the indigenous people of Jamaica was their lack of immunity to ailments and diseases brought by the Spaniards. Even the common cold was deadly and decimated the aboriginal population.

There are no Taino Arawak left in Jamaica. Signs of their existence only come to light when archaeologists discover their village sites or burial grounds. What little is known about Taino Arawak culture in Jamaica comes from the recorded observations of the Spaniards.

An artist's rendering of a carrack, a ship used in the 15th and 16th centuries by Europeans sailing the oceans.

THE SPANISH ARRIVAL

Europeans first sighted Jamaica in 1494. While they described the beauty of the island in glowing terms, it was not fields and mountains that attracted them to Jamaica. It was gold.

When the hunt for gold ended in vain, the Spaniards took comfort in the island's amazingly fertile soil. During the next 10 years, 80 Spanish ships a year on average sailed to the Caribbean, marking the start of European colonization in Jamaica.

By 1515 so few Taino Arawak were left on the island that the Spaniards began importing slaves from Africa. The Spanish settlers made money exporting cattle and cattle hides. By the beginning of the 17th century, the Spaniards had built a church and a monastery on the island.

Compared to the fabulous riches that the Europeans discovered elsewhere, Jamaica had little to offer. The Spaniards did not find gold on the island, but it was gold nonetheless that sustained their interest in the region. They regarded Jamaica only as a valuable supply base, and while some money could be made from agriculture, the real wealth crossing the Atlantic Ocean to Spain was gold taken from Mexico after the Aztec rebellion had been crushed. It was the wealth in gold that attracted other Europeans to the Caribbean. In 1655 the English army landed in Jamaica and ended Spanish rule.

CHRISTOPHER COLUMBUS

Christopher Columbus, or Cristoforo Colombo, was born in 1451 in Genoa, Italy. His lifetime ambition was to find a westward route to India and the Orient for trade in Asia's valuable spices. He made four trips across the Atlantic and visited Jamaica on two of them.

Although Columbus did not visit Jamaica on his first trip, he visited Cuba and heard stories of a gold-rich island called Xaymaca. On his second trip, he made it a point to visit and explore the island. He established contact with the inhabitants but found no gold.

Columbus' next trip to Jamaica was eight years later, in 1502. It was to be his last voyage across the Atlantic. His second visit to Jamaica proved to be unfulfilling. After a year exploring the Central American coast, his worm-eaten wooden ships became waterlogged and unfit for further travel. Columbus took refuge on the island of Jamaica, where he spent a year waiting to be rescued. During that time, he had to put down two rebellions by his own men. When he finally departed, there was no one left to go on calling the island Santiago—the name he had given it.

After returning to Spain in 1504, Columbus became very ill. He was also denied credit or recognition for his explorations. He died two years later, still thinking that he had successfully found an alternate route to India and the East. In 1540 the king and queen of Spain presented Columbus' family with Jamaica as a gift, although Columbus himself might not have been very pleased by the gesture in light of the unpleasant year he had spent on the island. For another 115 years, Jamaica remained a largely undeveloped Spanish colony, until the English attacked and conquered in 1655.

Caribbeans have strong negative feelings about the European impact on their history. In 1992, 500 years after Columbus arrived in the West Indies, countries in the Caribbean held parties and protests. To many people, Columbus was a symbol of the imperialism that overwhelmed indigenous Caribbean culture.

Fort Charles, named after King Charles II of England, is the oldest fortified site in Port Royal. It was used as a lookout for French and Spanish pirate ships trying to enter the harbor.

THE ENGLISH TAKEOVER

The 7,000 English soldiers who captured Jamaica in 1655 had actually been sent by the Crown to take the island of Hispaniola from Spain. When that mission failed, Admiral William Penn and General Robert Venables led their army on to Jamaica, which had already suffered many attacks by pirates and other European fleets. Villa de la Vega (present-day Spanish Town), the island's capital, was captured in less than two days.

THE MAROONS Land in Jamaica was given to the English soldiers and settlers, who became farmers. After invading Jamaica, the English became defenders of their new land, fighting off guerrilla attacks by the Spaniards and freeing African slaves.

Before the Spaniards fled from the English, they released and armed many African slaves, who raided English plantations periodically and assisted in numerous slave rebellions. These African-Jamaican guerrillas became known as Maroons, a name that may have been derived from the Spanish words *cimarrón* (see-ma-RON), meaning wild and untamed, or *marrano* (ma-RA-no), meaning wild boar. Descendants of the Maroons still live in Jamaica, and the Land of the Maroons is a region of the island.

Near Montego Bay, there is also an area known as the Land of Look Behind. The explanation for this goes back to the early days of English occupation when the English found themselves the targets of frequent surprise attacks by the Maroons. When they went out on patrol, they adopted the habit of sitting back-to-back on one mule. This was the only way they felt safe.

SIR HENRY MORGAN

The famous buccaneer Henry Morgan (1635–88) based himself at Port Royal, Jamaica, and helped make the island synonymous with piracy. The Welshman led raids on Spanish ships and looted Spanish settlements in Central America. In 1670 Morgan and his men even captured Panama.

A privateer, or licensed buccaneer, Morgan was knighted and appointed lieutenant-governor of Jamaica in 1674. He died in 1688 in Jamaica. Four years later, an earthquake destroyed most of Port Royal, including Morgan's burial site.

S⟨ HEN. MORGAN

"… lean, sallow-colored, his eyes a little yellowish and belly a little jutting out or prominent."

—Dr. Hans Sloane, describing the sick Henry Morgan in 1688, the year of his death.

NO PREY, NO PAY

During the 17th century Jamaican history was closely linked to the activities of pirates who preyed on Spanish ships sailing the Caribbean. The ships carried gold and treasure from Mexico and South America to Spain. The pirates were called buccaneers, derived from an indigenous word that meant to smoke meat. They were ruthless, violent men who murdered for a living, but their reckless courage created a glamorous, romantic image of them.

The buccaneers were mostly British and French. They made their headquarters at Port Royal in Jamaica. They kept their ships safe in the harbor, and the treasures that they stole from the Spanish ships created great spending power in the settlement, which prospered as a result.

Enemies of Spain, the buccaneers were valued by the British. Some, such as Henry Morgan, were called privateers. While their ships were privately owned, they were licensed by the British government to attack Spanish ships. The British government unofficially supported privateer activities until a treaty with Spain recognized Britain's right to hold possessions in the West Indies.

Legends of pirate treasures that sank to the bottom of the sea have fueled numerous diving expeditions attempting to recover the booty of Morgan and his fellow buccaneers.

THE PIRATES' HALL OF FAME

There were other buccaneers apart from Henry Morgan who gained a reputation in and around Jamaica, although they never enjoyed the same level of official recognition that eventually made Morgan a knight. On the contrary, many infamous pirates of the 18th-century West Indies were hunted to their deaths.

Edward Teach, better known as Blackbeard, was probably the most fearsome pirate of them all. He started his career in Jamaica. According to legend, Teach was a large man who went into battle with lighted matches plaited into his black beard and long hair. He died in 1718 in hand-to-hand battle.

Nicholas Brown stepped so far outside the law that a reward of £500, a vast sum at the time, was offered in Jamaica for his capture. In 1726 Brown was caught by John Drudge in Cuba. To secure the reward, Drudge cut off Brown's head and pickled it for the trip to Jamaica.

Captain Jack Rackham earned the nickname Calico Jack because of his fondness for calico underwear. When he was captured and brought to Jamaica for trial in 1720, it was discovered that two of his crew were women who had disguised themselves as men. It was said that the female pirates, Ann Bonney and Mary Read, were as rough and ruthless as their male counterparts. Rackham was executed in Port Royal, and his corpse was publicly suspended in an iron frame to serve as an example to those who might consider making a living from piracy. The place where Rackham's body was displayed, Deadman's Cay, was renamed Rackham's Cay.

SUGAR AND SLAVES

The Spaniards introduced sugarcane to Jamaica, and the English developed sugarcane production on the island because of the profit that could be made from exporting sugar to Europe. However, sugar production required a large labor force, which the population of Jamaica could not provide. By the 18th century, Taino Arawak had been wiped out, and most of the early African slaves had negotiated their freedom in the Maroon treaty of 1739.

Nevertheless, there was still an active slave trade. British ships traveled to the western coast of Africa to collect slaves and transport them to the West Indies. Jamaica became the main auction center where slaves were sold to the owners of sugarcane plantations on the island or sent to other colonies.

The sugar estates where the slaves were destined to spend the rest of their lives were like miniature towns. The owner lived on a hill, overlooking the sugarcane fields where the slaves labored and the plots of land on which they lived and cultivated their food crops.

In 1760 a former African chief, Tacky, led slaves in Jamaica in a revolt, but Tacky was shot and killed, and his men committed suicide. Only in 1831 did the Sam Sharpe rebellion precipitate the passing of the Slavery Abolition Act in 1833. However, the "freed" slaves were forced to continue working as poorly paid plantation "apprentices." Rebellions by the laborers and church groups ended apprenticeship in 1838. The slaves were finally fully free.

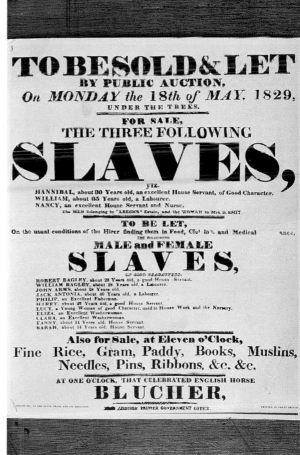

A notice announcing the sale of slaves like goods.

Donald Sangster, deputy prime minister, and Alexander Bustamante, prime minister, pictured with U.S. President John F. Kennedy in 1963.

TROUBLED TIMES

The abolition of slavery did not dramatically improve life for African-Jamaicans. Years into their new lives as free people, the former slaves faced great difficulty trying to break deeply entrenched social barriers. Thousands remained poor peasants.

Troubles mounted when the government and missionaries tried to prevent the African-Jamaicans from observing their traditional Christmas celebrations in 1841. A riot broke out. Many African-Jamaicans began to see religion as a weapon of oppression, although religion was also an instrument of development. They grew hostile to the very missionaries who had helped them attain freedom and who were still helping them establish their own communities.

Years after the riot, Jamaica's landowners, called planters, who had always dominated the House of Assembly, tried to protect their own interests. They resisted change, overworked the soil, and paid their workers meager wages. Worker rebellions plagued the island.

In 1865 poverty-stricken African-Jamaicans rebelled at Morant Bay, demanding improvements in their living and working conditions. The rebellion was ruthlessly crushed. Hundreds were executed, including two of the leaders, Paul Bogle and George William Gordon, who became national heroes. The House of Assembly was dissolved in 1866, and Jamaica became a Crown colony.

When the Great Depression hit Europe and the United States in the 1930s, the price of sugar plummeted, adding to the gloom in Jamaica. More outbreaks of violence worsened racial tension.

Out of the turmoil arose two individuals and two organizations that were to play crucial roles in Jamaica's future. Norman Manley founded the People's National Party (PNP) in 1938, and Alexander Bustamante organized a trade union that attracted dock workers and plantation laborers and, in 1943, developed into the Jamaica Labor Party (JLP). Manley and Bustamante pushed for social and political reforms, and in 1944 a new constitution declared for the first time the right of every Jamaican adult, regardless of color, to vote.

INDEPENDENCE

In 1958 Jamaica joined the West Indies Federation. Two years later, a referendum was held on the island's continued membership in the federation, which was beset with problems. The JLP campaigned for discontinued membership, which was the outcome.

A general election was held in April 1962. The JLP won not just the election but also the opportunity to head Jamaica's first independent government. On August 6, 1962, the flag of independent Jamaica was raised for the first time. Two weeks of celebration followed, as Jamaica became the 109th member of the United Nations.

"Independence wid a vengeance, Independence raisin' cain, Jamaica start grow beard, ah hope, We chin can sta' de strain."

—Louise Bennett, *expressing Jamaican pride on Independence Day in 1962*

GOVERNMENT

JAMAICA HAS BEEN INDEPENDENT since 1962, but it is one of 12 Caribbean countries that remain members of the Commonwealth of Nations and that recognize the Queen of England as their head of state. The commonwealth is made up of independent states that were once subjects of the British empire and that maintain friendly relations with the United Kingdom. Jamaica's governor-general is appointed by the Queen of England to represent her in the island state. The position is purely ceremonial, since it has no executive powers.

Jamaica is a parliamentary democracy, which means that it has a multiparty form of government with an executive branch and a privy counsel. For more than 50 years, Jamaica had only two major political parties: the Jamaica Labor Party (JLP) and the People's National Party (PNP). New parties such as the National Democratic Movement (NDM) were formed in the 1990s.

Jamaica's bicameral parliament consists of a House of Representatives and a Senate. The house of representatives has 60 members who are elected by popular vote for a five-year term. The Senate's 21 members are appointed by the governor-general. The party that wins the most votes in the general election appoints 13 members to the Senate, which ensures that it has a majority representation. The opposition gets eight seats.

Opposite: **The residence of the prime minister of Jamaica.**

Below: **Inside Jamaica's parliament house.**

ORGANIZATION OF THE JAMAICAN GOVERNMENT

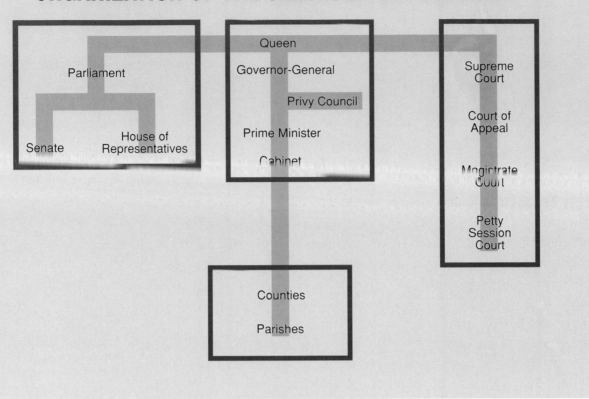

Parliament

Senate

House of
Representatives

Queen

Governor-General

Privy Council

Prime Minister

Cabinet

Supreme
Court

Court of
Appeal

Magistrate
Court

Petty
Session
Court

Counties

Parishes

PARLIAMENTARY DEMOCRACY

Bicameralism in Jamaica is a legacy of the island's colonial past. The Jamaican parliament is modeled after the British system. The House of Representatives, led by the prime minister, is the elected government and the main legislative body of the nation. The Senate's members are appointed rather than elected, and its decisions can be overruled by the House of Representatives. The Senate's main role is to debate and sanction legislation that is proposed by the House of Representatives. In 2003 Prime Minister Percival James Patterson announced Jamaica's intention to become a republic with an elected president by 2007.

Local government is run by elected councils, with grants from the central government for basic services. Three counties cover 14 parishes: Hanover, Westmoreland, Saint James, Saint Elizabeth, and Trelawny in Cornwall in the west; Manchester, Clarendon, Saint Ann, Saint Catherine, and Saint Mary in Middlesex in the center; and Saint Andrew, Kingston, Portland, and Saint Thomas in Surrey in the east.

Percival James Patterson, the leader of the People's National Party, was elected prime minister of Jamaica in 1992.

SEESAW POLITICS

Under Alexander Bustamante, the JLP held power for nine years after independence. Bustamante had a magnetic personality, and his ability to speak on the level of ordinary Jamaicans made him very popular.

In 1972 the PNP swept to power, and Michael Manley, Norman Manley's son, became prime minister. The younger Manley was a charismatic leader. A socialist, he initiated many economic and social reforms that set out to redress the inequality between rich and poor. Minimum wages were established, and the rights of trade unionists consolidated. Jamaica became an active member of the nonaligned movement, a group of governments opposed to the Cold War between the United States and the former Soviet Union.

Manley's sympathy toward Cuba and the Soviet Union added to the PNP's socialist policies and upset many business interests. Valuable international and U.S. aid began to diminish.

Such changes caused economic hardship for many Jamaicans, and in the 1980 election, the JLP returned to power and reversed many of the PNP's policies.

Jamaican police officers. The police force is called the Red Stripes because of the red seams decorating the officers' trousers.

THE SECOND JLP PERIOD The JLP made the biggest policy changes in foreign affairs. In 1980 the JLP leader, Edward Seaga, became the first head of state to visit the newly elected U.S. president, Ronald Reagan. When Reagan repaid the courtesy by visiting Jamaica in 1982, he became the first U.S. president to officially visit the island. The pro-U.S. stance of the JLP was also indicated by the closure of the Cuban embassy in Jamaica.

By 1989 Jamaicans realized that the JLP was getting no farther in managing the economy than the party they had replaced in 1980. In addition, the devastation caused by Hurricane Gilbert in 1988 resulted in a significant drop in export earnings from agriculture, mining, and services. Government spending on health and education was sharply reduced, and adverse economic conditions prevented the JLP from returning to power in 1989.

On March 30, 1992, Percival James Patterson, the leader of the PNP, became the first African-Jamaican to be elected prime minister.

THE MANLEYS

The People's National Party (PNP) was founded by Norman Manley (*right*) in 1938. The party led the nationalist campaign for independence from Britain, and it was Norman Manley, a lawyer, who drafted a revised constitution that paved the way for independence in 1962. Nevertheless, the Jamaica Labor Party (JLP), led by Alexander Bustamante, won the first election. Manley died before his own party won power in 1972.

Norman Manley and Bustamante are considered the fathers of modern Jamaica. Bustamante was Manley's cousin. In fact, three of Jamaica's first five prime ministers —Bustamante, Michael Manley, and Hugh Shearer—came from the same family.

Michael Manley, Norman Manley's son, became prime minister in 1972. He was a flamboyant politician whose rhetoric held audiences spellbound. He was given the biblical nickname Joshua and hailed the prophet-politician who would lead his country to salvation. His socialist policies, however, conflicted with those of the International Monetary Fund (IMF) and the Western allies. When the necessary loans could not be secured, Jamaica came close to bankruptcy. When Manley lost power in 1980, unemployment had risen to more than 30 percent. Manley accused the U.S. government of secretly destabilizing Jamaica because of his sympathy for Cuba and the Soviet Union.

After his defeat in 1980, Manley led a very determined opposition to the rule of the JLP. He continued to champion the rights of the poor, and his party's slogan for the 1989 election, "We put PEOPLE first," was in marked contrast to the JLP's slogan, "You need cash to care."

The difference between Manley's first and second governments (1972–80 and 1989–92) was very significant. In his second term of office, he worked amiably with the IMF and accepted the case for a free-market economy and curbs on government spending. Unfortunately, his health declined, and it came as no surprise when he passed the mantle of power to his deputy prime minister, Percival James Patterson, in 1992. Manley died in 1997, and the era of Manley politics, which had lasted for more than 50 years, finally came to an end.

Graffiti expresses Jamaicans' dissatisfaction with government policies.

POLITICAL VIOLENCE

Jamaicans are passionate about their country's politics. Unfortunately, their passion has in the past turned into violence on the streets. During the 1976 and 1980 elections, rival gangs belonging to the JLP and PNP conducted their campaigns not only with speeches but also with guns.

In 1976 a gang of political zealots machine-gunned the house where Bob Marley, the country's international reggae star, was staying. Marley survived the attack and later wrote about the assassination attempt in a song entitled *Ambush in the Night.*

In 1980 Marley again confronted political gangsters and called for peace. He held a concert at which he invited the leaders of the JLP and PNP to the stage to join in singing *One Love.* Despite such efforts, 1980 saw even more violence than 1976.

Jamaica's election violence scared not just locals but also tourists. As scenes of fighting and killing in Jamaica flashed across television screens around the world, people who were considering a vacation in

Jamaica changed their minds. A mainstay of the Jamaican economy, tourism was badly affected by the internal violence. However, since the 1970s and 1980s, political violence has lessened considerably.

HUMAN RIGHTS

The violence that has characterized Jamaican politics has led people elsewhere to think that the country's democratic foundation is weak. However, Jamaica has an excellent human-rights record, and there is widespread respect for civil rights.

The Jamaican legal system, like its government, is modeled on the British system. Justice is administered by a system of courts. There are small local courts, a court of appeal, and a Supreme Court, which is the final court of appeal. The judiciary functions as a separate arm of the government so as to shield courts as much as possible from political influence and enable them to uphold civil rights.

One exception was made in 1980, when a state of emergency was declared to curb election violence, and a Gun Court was set up with powers that curtailed some basic human rights. The special powers were aimed at controlling political gangsters who threatened to undermine the democratic system.

Several new human-rights organizations have been established in Jamaica in the first years of the 21st century. Jamaicans for Justice has achieved the greatest success in attracting international attention to human-rights abuses in Jamaica and acting as a general watchdog on Jamaican government security forces.

Jamaica continues to practice capital punishment. Britain's privy council, a final court of appeal for Jamaican courts, commutes death sentences more than five years old to life imprisonment.

The Jamaican constitution guarantees the rights of the individual with regard to free speech and movement. The individual is guaranteed the right not to be imprisoned without a fair trial.

ECONOMY

THE JAMAICAN ECONOMY has traditionally depended on agriculture, which still employs nearly 21 percent of Jamaica's workforce. Besides sugar, Jamaica's main crops are bananas, coffee, cacao, and citrus fruit. Jamaican rum, a by-product of sugar, is famous around the world and widely exported.

Mining and tourism are the island's main sources of income today. Mining employs a small percentage of Jamaica's workforce, but it is a crucial source of income. One of the most useful metals in industry, aluminum, is produced from a mineral compound that is extracted from bauxite. Versatile, lightweight, and resistant to corrosion, aluminum is easily worked and has a wide range of applications, from foil that is used for wrapping food to the body parts of aircraft and automobiles. Most of Jamaica's bauxite is sold to the United States and other industrialized nations to be processed into aluminum. Required by law to rehabilitate mined out land, bauxite companies in Jamaica spend large amounts of money to restore sites to pasture, forest, and agriculture.

Tourism plays a vital role in Jamaica's economy. It has enabled the country to diversify from agriculture, and today some 300,000 Jamaicans work in tourism-related industries. In 1981 the Jamaican government reorganized its tourism agencies to provide better service. Companies involved in tourism are also encouraged to consider the social and environmental effects of their activities.

Manufacturing exports earn Jamaica valuable foreign currency. The island's manufacturing industry has expanded beyond its traditional activities of food and mineral processing. Jamaican factories produce increasing volumes of clothes for export markets and account for 20 percent of the nation's total foreign exchange. Manufacturing as a whole employs 19 percent of the Jamaican workforce.

Opposite: **The processing of sugarcane involves the use of heavy machinery.**

MINING

Jamaica's most important mining industries are bauxite and gypsum. Jamaica is the world's second-largest producer of bauxite. The nation's bauxite deposits are generally found near the surface, making opencut, or strip, mining possible. While the opencut method is cost-effective, it severely damages and pollutes the environment.

Drilling and blasting machines are used to remove the topsoil and covering sand or clay. Gigantic mechanized shovels then scoop the exposed ore and load it onto heavy trucks to be transported to the processing facility. There, the mined ore is mixed with caustic soda and heated to form a solution. The solution is cleaned of impurities through the process of filtration. The filtrate then goes through precipitation to extract the alumina, or aluminum oxide, and calcination to burn off the

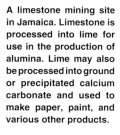

A limestone mining site in Jamaica. Limestone is processed into lime for use in the production of alumina. Lime may also be processed into ground or precipitated calcium carbonate and used to make paper, paint, and various other products.

moisture. The resulting product, white alumina powder, is very expensive to produce in Jamaica. The process requires a lot of electricity, and fuel for the island's power plants is mostly imported.

Gypsum occurs as crystals or, when fine-textured, as alabaster. The soft, fine texture of alabaster allows it to be sculpted and hand polished into vases. Gypsum is also calcined to make plaster of paris.

TOURISM

Windsurfing boats on the beach at Wyndam Rose Hall Hotel, Montego Bay.

Jamaica's congenial climate attracts visitors throughout the year, and resorts such as Montego Bay are internationally renowned. Most tourists come to Jamaica from the United States and Canada, but there are also many who travel from as far away as Australia or Japan. Tourism earns more foreign exchange than any other industry.

Some people question the real benefit of tourism to Jamaica, where most hotels are owned by foreign companies that often repatriate their profits, leaving little money for local development.

In addition, many Jamaicans have very low incomes, and the wealth of tourists, particularly those from the United States, emphasizes their poverty. Jamaicans who work in the tourist areas are constantly exposed to the glamorous lifestyles of foreigners, and the contrast with their own lifestyle can be a source of resentment.

Harvesting sugarcane with a machete is back-breaking work.

SUGAR

The sugarcane plant is a tall grass with a stout jointed stalk that stores sucrose, a natural sugar that is used in the food industry around the world. Jamaica's tropical climate provides the ideal conditions for the cultivation of sugarcane.

The economic value of sugar in the 17th and 18th centuries can be compared to that of oil in the 20th century. The immense wealth generated from sugar production made the Caribbean islands a precious part of the British empire.

In addition, the development of the sugar industry changed the cultural composition and social structure in the producer countries. A small elite group of rich European colonists owned the vast sugar plantations, while masses of poverty-stricken slaves from Africa worked the fields.

Today, while leading sugar producers such as the United States use machines to cut and harvest sugar, Jamaica still employs people to cut the cane manually, often using a machete. Cane harvesting and cutting is a physically demanding but poorly paid job.

Workers on sugarcane plantations in Jamaica face difficult economic conditions. In 1990 a journalist who visited an estate about 30 miles (48 km) west of Kingston reported that a 60-year-old sugarcane cutter took home only half of his $25 weekly earnings after deductions and taxes, and a 54-year-old woman on a nearby plantation was left with just $1 from her previous week's earnings of $17.

SUGAR PRODUCTION

After the sugarcane stalks have been washed and cut, they are passed through shredding and crushing machines that extract the juice from the stalk pieces. High-pressure water sprays help to dissolve the sugar from the stalks, producing greatly diluted cane juice. The crushed cane, or bagasse, is used to make chipboard and fuel.

The diluted cane juice is heated, filtered, and treated with lime to remove impurities. Carbon dioxide is later passed through the liquid to neutralize the lime. Sulfur dioxide lightens the color of the juice. The juice is sent to evaporation tanks, where most of the water is removed, leaving behind a thick syrup. Heating removes the remaining water in the syrup and facilitates the formation of sugar crystals.

The sugar crystals that form in the syrup are put into a centrifuge. The high-velocity spinning of the centrifuge separates the sugar crystals from the syrup. The separated components of the mixture are raw sugar, which is almost pure sucrose, and molasses, the residual syrup.

Raw sugar may be sold as the final product, or it may undergo additional diluting, filtering, evaporating, and spinning to produce white sugar. Molasses may become food for farm animals, especially dairy cows, or it may be distilled to produce rum.

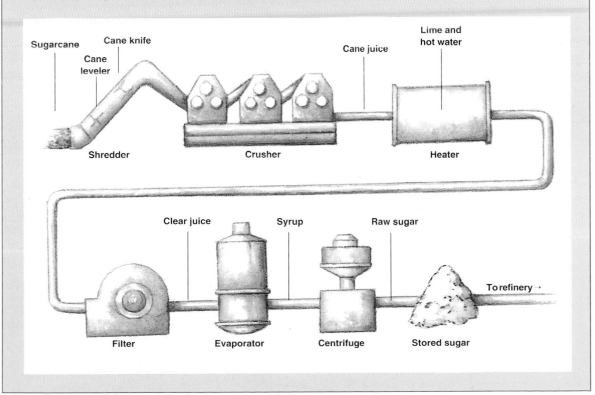

"What is needed now is teamwork, on a national level, to develop ... the remarkable fertility of the island ... This must go hand in hand with human development, for people are Jamaica's most valuable natural resource."

—Ken Maxwell,
West Indies Chronicle

ECONOMIC DIRECTION

Jamaica rebounded in the 1990s from the economic problems of the previous two decades, reducing unemployment by 25 percent and inflation to around 7 percent. The gross national product (GNP) per capita—the money value of goods and services produced divided by the population—rose from $1,340 in 1992 to $3,900 in 2002.

While Jamaica's economy has grown, its wealth has not been evenly distributed. Radical reforms in the 1970s to correct wealth inequity achieved little success. Critics allege that the country survived only because illegal marijuana shipments to the United States and the island's position as transit center for other illegal drugs earned Jamaica more money than legitimate exports did.

In the 1980s, foreign firms were encouraged to set up manufacturing plants in Jamaica, creating more than 30,000 jobs, especially in the clothing industry. However, wages remained low. Employees in a garment factory, for example, earned on average only slightly more than $10 a week after deductions, although the sweaters they produced would be priced five times higher in the United States. It soon became clear that the "free-market" policies brought little, if any, benefit to economically disadvantaged Jamaicans.

Emigration is another economic problem. Many Jamaicans move to other countries, some temporarily but others permanently, in search of better opportunities to realize their academic or career aspirations. Remittances from Jamaicans living abroad are second only to tourism in importance to the Jamaican economy. The Jamaican diaspora plays a big role in politics in major cities in the United States. The Jamaican government has attempted to draw from the skills of the diaspora to develop the economy back home.

The Jamaican government after 1992 achieved much greater success than its predecessors did in managing the economy. The budget deficit was considerably reduced, and the economy saw growth in many industries, such as tourism, bauxite, and manufacturing.

With greater political stability and decreased violence, Jamaican tourism has boomed, while a higher world market price for bauxite has improved prospects of investment in the mining industry. In 2003 bauxite production reached a record output of 13.5 million tons with projected earnings of $760 million. In manufacturing, areas that have expanded include clothing, footwear, and chemicals.

There have been setbacks. In 2001 Jamaican tourism suffered the economic aftershocks of the attack on the World Trade Center in New York. In 2002 the country had a foreign debt of about $4.7 billion.

Jamaica offers facilities and services for vacationers to enjoy beach activities and cruises along the coast. The future of Jamaican tourism depends largely on the preservation of the natural environment.

47

ENVIRONMENT

JAMAICA'S NATURAL ENVIRONMENT goes beyond turquoise waters and white beaches. The island is home to an abundance of plants, fish, birds, mammals, and insects, including many indigenous species. Because of the tremendous demand on the land especially due to tourism, this natural paradise is threatened by deforestation and pollution.

Opposite: **Dunn's River Falls in Ocho Rios.**

Jamaica is highly susceptible to nature's destructive forces because of its geographical location and geological history. However, it is humans who pose the biggest threat to the island's environment. Challenges Jamaicans face in preserving the country's fragile ecosystems include industrial pollution and heavy deforestation.

Pollution and deforestation severely damage Jamaica's forests, which like other natural ecosystems provide support for the very wildlife and wetlands that make Jamaica such a popular tourist destination.

Ironically, the tourist industry has been one of the greatest causes of pollution and deforestation in Jamaica. While tourism has contributed immensely to the economy, it has also accelerated environmental degradation, reducing the island's ability to sustain its tourist industry without the success of environmental preservation efforts.

INDUSTRIAL POLLUTION

Bauxite mining, a large source of foreign exchange for Jamaica, is one of the island's most destructive industries. To extract bauxite, vegetation and topsoil have to be completely removed. This exposes the soil to the eroding elements of the weather.

Also, for every ton of alumina extracted, a ton of caustic red mud residue seeps into the groundwater. This has caused the deterioration of watershed areas, not only threatening aquatic life but also limiting rural dwellers' access to sources of fresh water.

DEFORESTATION

According to the National Environmental Planning Agency (NEPA), Jamaica loses 16 percent of its forested area and up to 50 tons of topsoil to erosion every year. Deforestation in Jamaica has been linked mostly to agriculture and mining, but commercial development and expansion is also a culprit.

Almost 75 percent of Jamaica's original lowland forests have been cleared for agricultural purposes. Agriculture is an essential component of the economy. About half the island population earns an income from some form of agriculture.

In particular, the cultivation and export of consumables such as fruit, sugarcane, and coffee beans has helped boost the Jamaican economy. Blue Mountain coffee is a major source of income for the island. There is

A bauxite mining site in northern Jamaica shows the impact of extraction on the land.

a great foreign demand for it. However, as the coffee plantations expand, environmental problems such as soil erosion and the loss of wildlife habitat worsen.

ENDANGERED WILDLIFE

Four of the world's eight recognized sea turtle species live in Jamaica: the green, hawksbill, leatherback, and loggerhead turtles. All are in danger of extinction and are protected under Jamaican law. Hunters kill turtles for their shells and eggs. A sea turtle produces 80 to 200 eggs at a time during the nesting season, from May to October. It lays several batches each season but nests only every two to three years.

A man holds a young crocodile at the Safari Village in Montego Bay.

The American crocodile is one of 22 recognized crocodile species. This carnivore lives in the West Indies, north to the southern tip of Florida and south to Ecuador. It prefers coastal areas with high temperatures and inhabits mainly wetlands, lagoons, and rivers. It is becoming rare because of widespread hunting.

The Jamaican Hutia is a dark-brown rodent similar to the guinea pig. It lives mostly in the island's remote mountain regions and finds shelter in limestone holes. Its main diet consists of fruit, vegetables, and seeds. It has been hunted to extinction in much of its original habitat.

The black-billed and yellow-billed parrots get their names from the color of their bills. They make their nests in trees in the limestone forests of the John Crow Mountains and the Cockpit Country. Both parrots are vegetarian, feeding on fruit and nuts. Their population is decreasing because of habitat loss, illegal capture for the pet trade, and destruction by farmers who think that they are a threat to crops.

The beautiful greenery of Hope Gardens in Kingston attracts strollers, sightseers, picnickers, and birdwatchers.

NATURE'S HAVENS

Nature finds refuge in a few areas in Jamaica that have escaped tourist sprawl and maintained their beauty and richness. These include rivers, wetlands, hidden waterfalls, and wildlife preserves.

BLUE AND JOHN CROW MOUNTAINS NATIONAL PARK Jamaica's largest forest reserve is one of its most popular tourist attractions. Hundreds of plant, insect, and bird species reside in the tropical foliage and waterfalls of the Blue and John Crow mountains.

The giant swallowtail butterfly, with an amazing six-inch (15-cm) wingspan, lives in the high altitudes. Four types of hummingbird, the smallest birds on the island, live in the forest. The park is also home to the national bird—the legendary doctor bird, featured in many island stories and on the Jamaican two-dollar bill.

In addition, many exotic plants, including several varieties of orchids, thrive in the humid climate of the area. The national tree of Jamaica—

the Blue Mahoe—and many hardwoods, such as mahogany, can also be found in the park in abundance.

MONTEGO BAY MARINE PARK Jamaica's oldest national park was established in 1992 mainly to preserve coral reefs, seabed grass, and shoreline mangroves. Visitors to the 15-square mile (39-square km) park are allowed to fish, dive, play water sports, or collect shells only in designated areas so as to minimize environmental disturbance.

NEGRIL MARINE PARK Established in 1997 as part of efforts to protect the Negril watershed, the park includes the Great Morass swampland, an offshore lagoon, and coral reefs. There is a controlled-fishing area, and tourist activities are generally restricted to less environmentally harmful activities. A trust has been established to fund park maintenance.

The Great Morass is 125 square miles (324 square km) of wetlands in the small town of Black River. It is home to more than 100 species of bird, including seven types of heron. There are also about 300 American crocodiles living in the swamps.

COCKPIT COUNTRY NATIONAL RESERVE Considered the most rugged part of Jamaica, the Cockpit Country is 500 square miles (1,295 square km) of eroded limestone and rich foliage. In the 17th century, Maroons hid in the area to escape enslavement. Some areas of the perimeter of the reserve have been cleared for farming, but most of the Cockpit Country is unexplored, which is probably why it has remained relatively unspoiled.

The reserve is home to 27 endemic species, a few of which are endangered. The Jamaican government has plans to declare the Cockpit Country a national park.

CARIBBEAN CORAL REEFS IN DANGER OF EXTINCTION

Coral reefs support a variety of marine creatures, such as crabs, sponges, urchins, and fish. Reefs are made up of tubular sacs called polyps. The pigments of the polyps paint the reef a rainbow of colors, from bright reds and yellows to deep greens and purples. Some of the world's most beautiful reefs are found in Jamaica—Ocho Rios *(below)*, Montego Bay, and Discovery Bay.

There are many coral species around the world, even in the polar regions, but reef-building polyps need warmth. They thrive in tropical waters no more than 130 feet (40 m) deep, where sunlight can easily penetrate and temperatures range between 68 and 82°F (60 and 28°C). Coral reefs are important because they are home to marine creatures and remove carbon dioxide from the environment. They also protect coastal areas from hurricanes and floods.

In 2003 a group of British scientists did an extensive coral reef study. Based on 263 reef sites in the Caribbean, the study concluded that more than 25 percent of reefs in the tropics have been damaged or destroyed. Although coral reefs face natural marine predators, disease, and weather damage, their worst enemy is pollution in the form of hazardous chemicals, toxic waste, and garbage. Coral reefs are hardy and can live from decades to centuries, but they take a very long time to develop. Changes in Jamaica's environmental laws may not have come in time to save all of the island's coral reefs, but they can at least slow down the rate of reef destruction and help threatened coral species survive.

ENVIRONMENTAL PROTECTION

Jamaica's National Environmental Planning Agency (NEPA) was set up in 2001 to ensure that the island's natural resources are preserved and managed in an environmentally friendly way. But Jamaica's conservation efforts began before that, in the 1990s. NEPA and other environmental organizations encourage people to use clean sources of energy, such as hydroelectric and solar power. Farmers have also been educated about the proper use of pesticides, fertilizers, and other agricultural chemicals in attempts to improve farming and forestry methods and reduce soil erosion and watershed contamination.

More than 10 environmental holidays, such as National Wood and Water Day, remind Jamaicans and tourists alike of their environmental responsibilities. One example of the government's efforts to bring environmental damage to a halt is increased control of forest clearing, which recognizes that it is necessary to monitor the rate of clearing even though crops and lumber are important to the economy.

A home is nestled in the cliffs of Ocho Rios.

JAMAICANS

THE OVERWHELMING MAJORITY of Jamaicans are of African descent, but there is more of an ethnic mix than many people think. About 7.3 percent of Jamaicans are of mixed African-European origin.

After the abolition of slavery in 1838, there was a shortage of African laborers, so landlords and plantation owners turned to other countries for cheap replacements. Indian and Chinese laborers were imported into Jamaica.

In time, these migrants intermarried with African-Jamaicans, creating new minority ethnic groups. Today, there are significant African-Chinese and African-Indian minorities in Jamaica.

Left: **Jamaican boys of African descent.**

Opposite: **A fruit seller at the Montego Bay market.**

OUT OF MANY, ONE PEOPLE

Jamaica's national motto, engraved on the coat of arms, is "Out of Many, One People," translated from the Latin *Indus Uterque Serviet Uni.* The slogan reflects the island's mixed ancestry. Indeed, intermarriages have over centuries produced subtle shades in skin color among the Jamaican population.

Skin color has long been a basis for social discrimination in Jamaica. In the past, some mixed-race children were sent abroad by their European fathers for a private education. They then returned to elite positions in Jamaican society. Others got better jobs simply because they had lighter skin. In the 1950s African-Jamaicans held protests outside offices for the employment rights of African-Jamaican women, as certain workplaces, such as banks and retail stores, were employing only light-skinned women to serve their customers. The color prejudice could also be seen in churches. Europeans sat in the front pews, mixed-race individuals sat just behind them, and Africans filled the remaining seats to the back.

Many African-Jamaican women used to—and still do—use skin bleaching creams to lighten their complexion. In the 1960s and 1970s, at the height of the civil-rights and black-power movements in the United States, African-Jamaicans rediscovered a sense of pride in being black. However, bleaching creams made their comeback in the 1990s and are still widely used in Jamaica.

ETHNIC STATISTICS

Around 90 percent of the population of Jamaica is of African origin. The island's second largest ethnic group is of African-European descent. They make up slightly more than 7 percent of the population.

Most of the remaining Jamaicans—a little more than 1.3 percent of the population—are East Indians, and there are also Europeans, Chinese, and smaller ethnic minorities living on the island.

FROM SLAVES TO CITIZENS

It was a Spanish priest who, in 1515, first suggested to the Spanish government that Africans could replace the rapidly dwindling Taino Arawak laborers on sugarcane plantations in the Caribbean. European traders took their replacement laborers from coastal West Africa, from Senegal to the Congo. The African laborers who were taken to Jamaica became the ancestors of the majority of present-day Jamaicans.

Slaves continued to arrive in Jamaica long after the slave trade was abolished in the British colonies in the 1830s. For more than a century, economic and political power remained in the hands of non-African Jamaicans. Even after Jamaican independence in 1962, all three of the island's major sources of wealth—bauxite, sugar, and tourism—were under the control or influence of international corporations whose management did not include African-Jamaicans. In short, many African-Jamaicans who wanted to improve their position in society faced many social obstacles and deep-rooted prejudice.

In the 1970s the Jamaican government attempted to redress this imbalance. It inaugurated certain changes in the economy, the most significant of which was giving the state a degree of control over the island's bauxite industry and a share in the total production.

African-Jamaican movements resulted in changes with tremendous repercussions for African-Jamaican consciousness. Such movements continue to play an important role in the way contemporary Jamaicans perceive themselves.

Sugarcane cutters—a scene from Jamaica's past and present. A popular independence slogan, "Massa Day Done, Better Must Come," conveys the euphoria of Jamaicans freed from colonial servitude.

NEW AFRICAN-JAMAICAN CONSCIOUSNESS The Universal Negro Improvement Association (UNIA), founded by the Jamaican Marcus Mosiah Garvey in 1914, played a significant role in changing Jamaica's social and economic policies. The movement stressed the need for African-Jamaicans to shrug off the legacy of slavery and reassert their cultural identity and individuality.

Garvey's ideas were the spiritual force behind the Rastafarian movement. He also influenced African leaders in other countries, such as Malcolm X in the United States and Kwame Nkrumah, the first prime minister of Ghana.

The world's largest pan-African nationalist organization, the UNIA continues to work for the welfare of African peoples around the world.

MARCUS MOSIAH GARVEY (1887–1940)

When Marcus Mosiah Garvey founded the Universal Negro Improvement Association (UNIA) in 1914, the title sounded grandiose for a small group proclaiming that blacks would never achieve justice as long as whites dominated the ruling class. "Back to Africa" was the rallying call for the movement's belief that African peoples should return to their African homelands.

Garvey's organization did not initially attract many in Jamaica. In 1916 he went to the United States to spread his ideas, and by the 1920s he had more than 12 million followers worldwide. Contributions flowed in, and the money was used to help set up all-African businesses, part of Garvey's campaign for self-reliance and independence from a white-dominated economic system.

In 1925 Garvey was convicted of fraud in connection with the sale of stock in one of the businesses he had established. He was deported from the United States in 1927. He returned to Jamaica and attempted to enter national politics. In 1935 he left his family and moved to London, where he lived in obscurity until his death in 1940. On November 10, 1964, Garvey's body was returned to Jamaica and buried. The next day, he was declared the country's first national hero. His body lies in Kingston's National Heroes' Park in the Marcus Garvey Memorial.

A direct descendant of the slaves freed by the Spanish.

MAROONS

Although the original Maroons in Jamaica were slaves who were freed by the retreating Spanish colonists, the word maroon is a general word for runaway slaves.

When the English attacked the Spanish colony of Jamaica in the 17th century, the African slaves, numbering perhaps 1,500, were released and armed in a final attempt to fight the English. After the Spaniards fled, the slaves remained behind and joined the slaves who had earlier escaped to the mountains. In time, yet more slaves escaped from the plantations of the English, and for many years the Maroons conducted a guerrilla campaign against the new masters.

Maroon communities developed wherever plantations of slave labor existed. The Maroons of Jamaica are particularly noteworthy because of their independent status since the 18th century. While in the past this meant that they were free individuals in a slave community, today they are independent of government control, instead governing themselves.

The 18th-century Maroons found protection in the rugged terrain of the Blue Mountains and the Cockpit Country. The harsh environment kept their population low, but their determination never to surrender ensured that they remained a thorn in the side of the slave owners. Eventually, in 1739, the government made a treaty with the Maroons in the Cockpit Country, granting them 1,500 acres (607 hectares) of land and the right to self-rule. The Maroons were also given a license to hunt within 3 miles (5 km) of the town boundaries and to sell their produce in the markets.

One reason for the survival of the Maroons in the 18th century, apart from their strong sense of independence, was the isolation of the Cockpit Country. However, roads have made the area accessible, and modern influences have weakened the Maroons' sense of separateness. For example, they are more likely to find employment opportunities outside of the Cockpit Country.

Accompong has been one of the main Maroon villages in the Cockpit Country since the 18th century and is a pilgrimage site for Maroons from all over the island on Cudjoe Day (January 6). This day commemorates the signing of the peace treaty with the English when Cudjoe was the leader of the Maroon community in the Cockpit Country. The Maroons are gradually being integrated into the economic and social mainstreams of Jamaican life, but their unique history and character are being preserved.

No one really knows the total number of Maroons in Jamaica. estimates vary between 4,000 and 5,000.

ETHNIC MINORITIES

After the emancipation of Jamaica's slaves in 1838, plantation owners turned to cheap European labor. Ships called at ports in countries such as Ireland, promising migrants to Jamaica attractive rewards, such as "a sow pig and the milk of a cow for each family." Most of the recruits, including the Irish and some Portuguese, became field laborers. Some Scots and the English worked in skilled departments on sugar estates.

Jamaicans of different complexions—the result of successive generations of mixed unions.

Certain names in Jamaica bear testimony to the arrival of Germans on the island, for example, place names such as Saxony, Bohemia, and Berlin, and family names such as Wedermeyer and Eldermayer. Almost all the Germans who settled in Jamaica crossed the Atlantic as a result of the efforts of William Lemonius, who negotiated with an English landlord, Lord Seaford, for a grant of farming land. The peasants from the Rhineland worked as farmers in Jamaica and eventually intermarried with the indigenous population. Like the Scottish and the Irish, the Germans arrived in Jamaica shortly after the slaves were freed. The few families of German descent still living in Jamaica no longer speak German.

There is also a distinct Indian presence and influence in Jamaican society. The first Indian laborers arrived around the same time as the poor Europeans. Many of Jamaica's Indians are Christian, but some are Muslim or Hindu and celebrate their own festivals. The Indian influence can also be appreciated in the number of curry dishes in Jamaican cuisine. Curried goat, a popular dish at any Jamaican feast, originated in India. Marijuana also came from India.

NATIONAL DRESS

Jamaican dress is generally conservative but often brightly colored. Hats are popular with men and women. Women can be seen wearing broad, white, floppy hats and formal dresses on Sundays. Their Afro hairstyle reflects an African influence.

The crocheted cotton hat, or tam, is worn by many men, in particular by Rastafarians. The most spectacular feature of Rastafarian male dress, however, is the hairstyle, called dreadlocks. The hair is washed regularly but is not cut or styled. It is left to grow naturally and form locks on its own.

Dreadlocks originated among the Masai warriors and Ethiopian peoples of eastern Africa. The Rastafarians give a religious reason for letting their hair grow. They quote a phrase in the Bible that says that a person who has made a special vow "must let the hair of his head grow long" (Numbers 6:5).

MINORITY CONTRIBUTIONS Jamaica's ethnic minorities have made many important contributions to Jamaican society. The first Chinese immigrants were brought to the island around 1860 to work on the railroad. Today, Jamaica has a prominent Chinese community. The national football stadium was designed by Wilson Chong, a Jamaican of Chinese descent.

Lebanese, known as Syrians, have become a local capitalist class concentrated in the retail, horse-racing, and manufacturing industries in Jamaica. The Lebanese also introduced Syrian bread, a popular flat bread that has become an important staple in Jamaican cuisine.

The Lebanese first came to the island in the 1890s when Lebanon was still part of the Ottoman empire. Their number and influence in Jamaica have grown considerably over the years. One Lebanese, Edward Seaga, was prime minister of Jamaica from 1980 to 1989.

LIFESTYLE

PATTERNS OF LIFE in 21st-century Jamaica originate in the plantation society of 18th century Jamaica. The pace of life is generally laid-back and has been described as "soon-come-ism," a Creole phrase that says it does not really matter much if you put off until tomorrow what does not have to be done today.

FAMILY LIFE

Family life in Jamaica is centered more around the mother-child relationship than around the husband-wife relationship. Children, not marriage, mark a woman's passage to adulthood. This system of family organization has its roots in history.

Although slavery was abolished more than 150 years ago, the forms and patterns of family life that emerged during the era of slavery still influence present-day Jamaican society. Marriage between slaves was not recognized, and the father was not considered an integral member of the family.

Even today, if a man leaves his family, his children will stay with their mother and her extended family. The woman thus plays a central and decisive role in the family. She has access to birth control and will have children when she wants them. Primary health-care clinics provide prenatal and postnatal services for mothers and children.

The tradition of female self-reliance has also been nurtured and sustained by contemporary economic factors. For example, women are no longer confined to secretarial or clerical jobs but work in free-trade zones and in tourism as well. Also, many men leave the family to work abroad and earn higher wages. This is particularly true in rural areas, where good jobs are harder to find and women often shoulder the responsibility of bringing up the children.

George Lamming, a West Indian novelist, succinctly summed up the reality of family life in these memorable words: "my mother who fathered me ... my father who had fathered only the idea of me."

Opposite: **A Jamaican family eating at a restaurant.**

GROWING UP AND WORKING

A Jamaican child spends most of his or her growing-up years with the mother and sees little of the father, who may be working far from home. When they finish school, many young Jamaicans, especially males, go to Kingston to find jobs. They may work in a garage or help a relative at a market stall, and earn an average salary of around $20 a week.

Young Jamaican women who have finished formal education may work in various sectors of the economy, such as health care, the civil service, or free-trade zones, where multinational corporations have factories manufacturing clothing, footwear, and other goods. The 1975 Employment Act guarantees equal pay for equal work. This is true for jobs in the civil service, but women tend to be the first to be dismissed in times of economic depression.

Many young Jamaicans frequently change jobs. There is also the lure of finding work abroad. More than one million Jamaicans live in other countries, mostly in the United States.

MARRIAGE

Jamaican weddings are big celebrations involving a lot of expense and preparation. Before the wedding, the parents of the young man and woman have a formal meeting. Presents from friends and relatives start arriving long before the wedding day, sometimes months in advance. A common gift is eggs to be used to make the wedding cake. The grandmothers of the couple traditionally help to choose the couple's clothes for the ceremony.

On the night before the wedding, most guests will stay up singing and eating. The church ceremony is an occasion for everyone to dress in their best clothes. The ceremony is fairly short and is followed by

The relative rarity of legal marriages in Jamaica does not mean that people fail to establish lasting unions. The main obstacle is financial constraint. Many simply cannot afford the expense of a wedding and setting up a home.

the cutting of the wedding cake, which is typically a fruit cake filled with raisins, currants, and other fruit soaked in rum and wine. Speeches are then made before the happy event ends with a large feast and more merrymaking that continues into the early hours of the morning.

A wedding photo session in a garden in Jamaica. The island is a wedding-and-honeymoon location for couples from other countries as well.

FUNERALS

In Jamaica, a funeral, like a marriage, is a public event. Grieving for the loss of one's loved ones is not something confined to the privacy of the home. The coffin is likely to be placed on the verandah of the family's home, with the face of the deceased revealed by an opening in the top of the coffin. Relatives, friends, and neighbors visit to pay their respects, and some join in the wailing that customarily expresses the family's grief.

There is a belief in Jamaica that a man should not see his wife's coffin as it is being placed in the ground. It is believed that if he does and then remarries, his second wife will die early.

LIFESTYLE STATISTICS

Jamaica's infant mortality rate was around 13 deaths per 1,000 live births in 2003. The rate was higher for boys (around 14 deaths per 1,000 live births) than for girls (around 12 deaths per 1,000 live births).

The average life expectancy of Jamaicans was around 76 years in 2003, with men living on average slightly shorter lives (74 years) than women (78 years).

More than half of Jamaica's almost 2.7 million people live in towns.

Around 82 percent of all Jamaicans can read and write.

Jamaica's low birth rate of around 17 births per 1,000 people in 2003 is largely the result of family-planning programs introduced in the 1970s and 1980s, when young women were encouraged to "Plan Your Family. Better Your Life." The fertility rate in 2003 was around two babies born to every woman.

Jamaica's mortality rate was around 5 per 1,000 people in 2003.

Jamaicans can legally marry after their 18th birthday, but most marry only after their 30th birthday. The Registrar General's Department records all marriages.

Jamaica has a divorce rate of around 0.5 per 1,000 people.

RURAL LIFE

Rural Jamaica was once a vital part of an economy that relied heavily on agriculture, namely the export of sugar and bananas to the United States and Europe. The prices of such produce plunged drastically in the 1930s, during the Great Depression, reducing the income of many Jamaican small farmers. Several hurricanes in the 1930s and imported crop diseases added to the difficulties, and young Jamaicans began to drift from the rural areas to towns in search of employment.

Today, the typical Jamaican farm is less than 5 acres (2 hectares) in size and tends to be self-sufficient. Yams are commonly cultivated. Yam plants are broad-leafed climbers, and farmers provide stakes for them to climb. The underground tubers of the yam plant are harvested for their starch-rich content. The tubers are peeled and then boiled or roasted and eaten like potatoes. Yam has a distinctly slimy feel and turns brown fairly quickly if it is not kept in water. In the United States, sweet potatoes, another genus, are sometimes called yams.

Other common crops cultivated on small farms in Jamaica include plantains, mangos, and cassava. The plantain is a type of banana that, unlike the variety commonly eaten raw, requires cooking to prepare its hard flesh for eating.

Small farmers in Jamaica may also keep chickens, pigs, and goats. They sell surplus fruit, vegetables, and livestock at the local market for cash, and this provides a source of income for their families.

In rural Jamaica, children help their parents with chores such as fetching water from the village tap.

URBAN GHETTOS

The urban areas of Jamaica continue to grow as more and more people leave the countryside to seek a better life in the cities. Rural-to-urban migration adds to the problem of housing.

In 1975 the Jamaican government established a housing corporation and trust to deal with the influx of low-income families into Kingston and other cities. Low-interest home-improvement loans as well as financing for new housing are funded by compulsory employer and employee subscriptions. The amount of money such schemes have at their disposal varies with the general state of the economy. Although the Jamaican economy has improved, ghettos continue to be a feature of urban life. Kingston, in particular, suffers in this respect, with thousands of people living in corrugated-iron shacks.

A slum area in Ocho Rios. Ghettos are a prominent feature in and around towns and cities, where there is a shortage of affordable housing.

The ghettos are home to Jamaica's urban gangs, which flourish in the harsh economic climate of deprivation. Many gangs have their roots in the gangs attached to rival political parties in the 1970s and early 1980s. Ghetto gangs focus on the drug trade but maintain political ties. The powerful gangster leaders are known as "top rankin" or "mos' wanted."

Concern about urban violence surfaced in 1987 after the murder of Peter Tosh, a reggae musician. The same year, a high-ranking supreme court judge was assassinated. In 1992 Kingston's slums became a battleground between rival gangs and the police after 40,000 people attended the funeral of a man alleged to have been involved in one of the more prominent gangs. More than a dozen people died in the showdown, and many were injured. Politically influenced gang violence erupted again in 2001, and Prime Minister Patterson ordered more than 3,000 troops into the area to control the violence.

A fruit and vegetable seller does business in a little corner of town.

On the corner of Kingston's King and Duke streets.

LIFE IN KINGSTON

Because Jamaica is a small island, its capital, Kingston, plays a bigger part in the lives of Jamaicans than perhaps London does in the lives of Britons or Washington, D.C., in the lives of Americans. Kingston is a mecca for young Jamaicans, who flock there hoping to find fame, maybe as the world's next reggae star, but often they are lucky to find any work at all. Most of the country's important national events take place in Kingston.

There is a visible distinction and demarcation in Kingston between the affluent minority, who aspire to a North American lifestyle, and the poor majority, who have low-income jobs or no regular employment. Yet, as many social commentators have noted, it is from the economically least-advantaged parts of the city that a cultural dynamic spills over to the rest of the country.

The government has made some effort to improve the living conditions of disadvantaged groups. For example, Tivoli Gardens, one of the more famous areas of Kingston, was once a slum area known as Back o' Wall. It was transformed into a lively community with the establishment of a health clinic, a maternity center, and numerous recreational facilities. Its carefully painted murals point to its youth and their cultural energy.

Schoolboys take a break
between classes.

EDUCATION

For a long time, only privileged white children in Jamaica had access to
the private schools run by various churches. Since independence, the
Jamaican government has worked to make education universal. Today,
education is compulsory and free for all Jamaican children ages 6 to 15,
the result of a 10-year education plan achieved with financial aid from
the World Bank, the United States, and Canada.

Kindergarten prepares children for entry into more formal schooling.
The government pays the teachers' salaries, but it is up to each parish
to provide suitable school buildings. Around 90 percent of all eligible
Jamaican children go to elementary school. Slightly more than half of all
those who are eligible attend high school, as the dropout rate increases
dramatically after the age of 12 or 13.

In many countries in the Caribbean, the education system is partly the
product of education during colonial rule. Jamaica still uses the British
educational system.

Jamaican girls have equal opportunities to obtain an education. Many do well and further their studies at the University of the West Indies or universities abroad.

BASIC EDUCATION English is the language of instruction in Jamaican schools. Children take a compulsory comprehensive examination soon after they turn 10. Based on their results, some children are selected for entry to prestigious government-aided high schools. The majority of children, however, transfer to their local comprehensive (junior high) school, where at the end of the third year they take a curriculum-based National Assessment Program (NAP).

The main academic examination is the British General Certificate of Education at Ordinary Level, or GCE "O" levels, taken at age 15 or 16. In addition, the Caribbean Examination Council organizes various other examinations that offer technical and commercial certification.

At age 18, the more academically inclined students take the GCE Advanced Level examination, and those who do well enter college. Less than 3 percent of Jamaican students take the GCE "A" levels. Unless a student was selected for a high school at age 10 or transferred to a high school from a comprehensive school, he or she is unlikely to take the GCE "A" level examination.

VOCATIONAL AND HIGHER EDUCATION Vocational schools train students in fields such as carpentry, metalwork, and home economics. Jamaica has 12 teacher-training colleges and 14 community colleges. Other education facilities include colleges for agriculture or technology, a dental auxiliary school, and a cultural training center that specializes in fine art, music, and dance. Graduates of such colleges are recognized as specialists in their chosen subject.

Jamaica is home to one of the three campuses of the University of the West Indies, founded in 1948. The other two campuses are located in Barbados and Trinidad. The Jamaican campus is situated just outside Kingston. It began with only 32 medical students and today boasts a population of more than 8,000 students from Jamaica and neighboring islands. The university was at the forefront of a 1970s movement that emphasized the need for West Indians to discover their cultural roots. Research, publications, and courses aimed to redress the imbalance caused by centuries of European domination were developed.

A well-recognized alternative for higher education in Jamaica is the University of Technology, formerly the College of Arts, Sciences, and Technology (CAST).

PRIVILEGED EDUCATION Adult illiteracy was a major problem in Jamaica after independence. The Jamaica Movement for the Advancement of Literacy (JAMAL) has been successfully improving literacy, running classes for more than a quarter million Jamaicans in 20 years.

At the other end of the educational spectrum are the private schools attended by children from wealthy families. Jamaica's private schools tend to be denominational, with a large number of expatriate teachers. Some wealthy Jamaicans send their children to other countries, mostly to the United States, for their studies.

Of all Jamaicans age 25 or older, some 19 percent have had no education, more than 75 percent have completed elementary school, more than 5 percent high school, and 0.5 percent have post-secondary education.

The *cannabis sativa* plant, better known as ganja in Jamaica.

MARIJUANA

Smoking marijuana, or ganja, is a part of the lifestyle of young people, especially young men, in Jamaica. The marijuana plant is not indigenous to the Caribbean but was introduced by Indian laborers imported in the last century.

It is illegal to smoke ganja in Jamaica, although a visitor to the island might easily think otherwise. It is common to see ganja smokers among spectators at a sporting event or in a cinema audience, and Rastafarians smoke ganja during their religious rituals. Many consider marijuana a general tonic and add it to their tea and cake batter.

Thousands of Jamaicans are employed in the growing, harvesting, and preparation of marijuana in the more remote rural regions of the country. Most of the harvest is flown to the United States from illegal airstrips scattered around the island. The authorities have tried to clamp down on these activities, but in a country where there is high unemployment and low wages, the temptation to get rich by cultivating marijuana is great.

It is common knowledge that professionals and otherwise respectable figures are also involved in the business as there are large profits to be made by exporting the crop to the United States.

Official attitudes toward the use of the drug have varied over the last 30 years. Shortly after independence, the law said that anyone caught growing the plant could be imprisoned, but this law has since been repealed. Various proposals have been made to legalize the drug for personal use so that ganja would be seen as just another crop, like tobacco for cigarettes or hops for beer, so that the price would fall and little profit would be made in pursuing its cultivation.

In the meantime, ganja continues to be illegal, and the police continue to try to clamp down on the export trade by raiding farms and closing down private airstrips where large quantities are flown overseas. The maximum sentence for the cultivation of ganja is a fine of up to $1,120 or a jail sentence of up to 10 years or both.

Ganja, although illegal, is sacred to Rastafarians for healing suffering and raising consciousness. The chalice pipe is the symbol of brotherhood.

RELIGION

THE AFRICAN SLAVES in Jamaica were not allowed to practice their own religion. This was not simply because the slave owners believed that Christianity was more meaningful but because a policy of religious intolerance was one way of breaking down the cultural identity that united the slaves in the face of oppression. The slaves were also taught to reject their original beliefs and to accept their subservience with humility.

However, the African religions did not die out. The missionaries adapted some of the traditional beliefs of the Africans and incorporated them into their teachings. The slaves accepted Christianity at face value but used it as a way to continue practicing their own traditional rituals.

Today, Christianity flourishes in Jamaica in various forms alongside other faiths that represent a hybrid of Christianity and African animism. Jamaica's own unique religion is Rastafarianism, and there are also small communities of Jews, Hindus, and Muslims.

Above: **An Anglican church in Falmouth.**

Opposite: **The interior of a church in Port Antonio.**

CHRISTIANITY IN JAMAICA

More than 60 percent of Jamaicans practice Christianity. Church services in Jamaica have been adapted to suit the island's pre-Christian culture of lively, music-filled worship. Members of the congregation participate actively in church services in Jamaica. There is almost always music, played on an electric organ or a tambourine, and singing can break out spontaneously among the congregation.

A Christian cemetery in Newcastle.

CHRISTIAN GROUPS There are more than 100 Christian denominations in Jamaica. Most are Protestant, mainly Baptist, Methodist, or Anglican.

The Baptists first came to the island in the 1780s, after the American War of Independence. The first Methodist missionary, the Reverend Coke, arrived on the island in 1789, but the Coke chapel was closed down the following year by the authorities, who objected to the political implications of his work with slaves.

The Baptists and the Methodists were instrumental in the conversion of large numbers of slaves. They were particularly successful because of their objection to the practice of slavery and their willingness to support the campaign for its abolition.

Roman Catholicism came to Jamaica with the first Spanish conquerors and today is practiced in Jamaica mainly by the Chinese and Indians.

There are also many smaller Christian groups in Jamaica, including the Seventh-Day Adventists, the Church of God, and the United Church of Christ. Christian fundamentalist groups are growing in popularity in Jamaica. Most of the fundamentalists came to the island from the United States. Many of the sects place strong emphasis on gospel singing and powerful sermonizing that admonishes the faithless and celebrates the rewards of the new faith.

ANIMISM

Animism is a belief based on the idea that animals, plants, and even inanimate objects have souls. The word animism comes from the Latin word *anima* (AH-nee-mah), meaning soul. The main belief of animism is that spirits can influence human events. Animistic religions came to Jamaica with the African slaves, and despite being banned by the European powers, they never completely disappeared from Jamaica's spiritual landscape.

Jamaica's African heritage is most apparent in the spirit religions. One of the most important is the *kumina* (KOO-mi-nah), where worshipers invoke deceased family members. The process of calling up ancestral spirits relies heavily on drums that help create a trance-like state. Two types of drums are used: the big *kimbanda* (kim-BAHN-dah), which produces a bass sound; and the small *kyas* (kee-yahs), which produces a treble sound. The use of music and dance in *kumina* worship is part of a Congolese religion.

In rituals associated with animism, the participant is often in a trance and does not feel pain when stepping on broken glass and other sharp objects.

KUMINA The *kumina* religion is celebrated as part of the national heritage. Some people turn to *kumina* rituals in the belief that spiritual forces can cure their illnesses or protect them from enemies. The main ritual is very dramatic. *Kumina* drums are showered with alcohol. The chief priestess sings a hymn and performs a ritual that has been passed down through generations from the African communities centuries ago. The priestess is credited with special spiritual powers that put her in a trance and enable her to communicate with the spirits. The sacrifice of an animal, usually a goat, is also a part of the ritual.

The *kumina* is one of the most popular pieces performed by the National Dance Theater Company of Jamaica, and it is also featured in festivals sponsored by the Jamaica Cultural Development Commission. The Swift River Bussu Festival in Chelsea, Portland, celebrates the local culture and the Bussu snail for a day every August with *kumina* drum music among other fun activities.

SUPERSTITION Ordinarily, the animistic element in Jamaican religious beliefs reveals itself only in popular superstition. The "rollin' calf" is one of the spirits in Jamaican folklore that is said to have the habit of moving around by night dragging a chain. It is believed that the spirit can kill farm animals, and farmers may hang a bottle on a nearby tree to protect their livestock from the "rollin' calf."

POCOMANIA AND REVIVAL ZION

So prevalent and significant is the influence of animism in Jamaica that it reaches beyond the practice of the original African rituals of *kumina* to create a unique hybrid religion. Where Christian and animistic beliefs and practices have merged, the resulting faith is known in Jamaica as Pocomania. Adherents meet to participate in a ceremony with the hope that they will be possessed by the spirit of God. The dialect word for the cult is *puckamenna*, and the religious dancing is described as "dancing the puckoo."

A Pocomania ceremony is centered on a long table covered with a white cloth. On it are bowls and plates of food lighted by candles. The almighty spirit is then invoked through song and dance. There is evangelistic preaching, followed by chanting and the singing of hymns. Powerful rhythms encourage the congregation to join in to attain a state of grace. Members of the congregation leave their places to begin a slow dancing march around the table, following a leader whom they call the shepherd if a man or mother if a woman.

Possession by a spirit is marked by frenzied singing or groaning, or perhaps speaking in tongues. Pocomanians believe that after such a possession, the spirit remains with the person as a kind of guardian angel who can be consulted for advice and guidance.

Revival Zion is a smaller sect resulting from the mixing of African and Christian traditions in Jamaica. It shares many similarities with Pocomania, such as dancing and spirit possession.

The Pocomanian altar is laden with offerings of flowers, candles, and food.

The Ethiopian Emperor Haile Selassie in 1968.

RASTAFARIANISM

Rastafarianism is a quasi-Christian religion that draws inspiration from the Old Testament and the Book of Revelations in the Bible, the speeches of Haile Selassie I, the prophecies of Marcus Garvey, and the lyrics of reggae musicians Bob Marley, Peter Tosh, and Bunny Walker. Rastafarians believe that their religion has no origin and has always existed, but it is generally agreed that Marcus Garvey, who emphasized the autonomy of black consciousness, was of pivotal importance in the growth of Rastafarianism.

Garvey was born in St. Ann's Bay, Jamaica, in 1887 and grew up in a society based on color differences. When Garvey left Jamaica for the United States in 1916, he was reported to have said, "Look to Africa when a black king shall be crowned; he shall be your Redeemer." Also, there were some who believed that Ethiopia was the promised land.

When Haile Selassie was crowned the emperor of Ethiopia in 1930, Rastafarians saw the fulfilment of Garvey's prophecy and revered Selassie as God. The name of their religion is derived from the title Selassie bore before he became emperor—Ras Tafari, which means crown prince in Amharic, the main language of Ethiopia.

After Garvey's death, Leonard Howell established a collective in Jamaica for more than 1,500 followers. The most distinctive physical feature of the Rastafarians then emerged—the dreadlock hairstyle that boldly proclaimed their Africanness.

Rastafarians, or Rastas, believe in the ubiquity and divinity of God, whom they call Jah. They believe that the spirit of Jah will help oppressed people to a heaven on earth. Rastafarians observe dietary laws similar to those of the Jews, excluding foods such as pork from their diet. Rastafarians also avoid milk and coffee, and many do not drink alcohol. As with nearly all religious communities in Jamaica, Rastafarians integrate music into their faith. In fact, reggae music developed within a Rastafarian context and produced the famous reggae star Bob Marley. The rhythm that forms the backbone of reggae music is the Rastafarian heartbeat rhythm known as Nyabinghi.

There are a few sects of Rastafarianism in Jamaica, the oldest being the Boboshanti, whose members, the Bobos, wear turbans and long cloaks and live in small communities that try to be economically self-sufficient.

The Twelve Tribes is most famous for having Bob Marley as one of its members. The group is characterized by a stronger political element than the other groups and champions the cause of working class Jamaicans.

Another Rastafarian sect is the Ethiopian Zion Coptic Church, which many members of the other sects look down on, partly because it is willing to engage in the commercial distribution of marijuana.

The number of Rastafarians worldwide is estimated to be more than one million, and Rastafarianism remains a vibrant religious force in Jamaica. The religion has spread to other islands in the Caribbean and to communities in the United Kingdom, the United States, Africa, and beyond, but the dynamism of Rastafarianism continues to be based on a strong sense of African pride.

Kumasi, an internationally known reggae singer, sports dreadlocks, the mark of Rastafarianism.

LANGUAGE

JAMAICA'S OFFICIAL LANGUAGE IS English, a legacy of the island's British colonial history. When slaves were brought to Jamaica from Africa, they were forced to learn English, which resulted in a linguistic blend known as Jamaican Creole. Patois

The slaves spoke English with the intonation and speech patterns of their own African languages. They found it difficult to pronounce sounds that did not exist in their languages and adopted the nearest equivalent. In trying to produce the "th" sound, for example, "the" became "de," "then" "den," and "that" "dat." ⇒ p.93, 101

Above and opposite: **Signs in Jamaica convey their messages in the nation's official language.**

The African slaves communicated with the British masters using this adapted form of English that followed their own intonation and speech patterns. African languages, in particular Twi, formed the backbone of the Jamaican patois, or local dialect, which developed over a period of time with not only a different way of pronouncing words but also a modified vocabulary.

Jamaican English vocabulary might give the impression that the islanders have been caught in a time warp. They have preserved some words and phrases found only in Shakespeare's works or in the Bible. Saying goodbye, for example, a Jamaican speaking patois may say "Peradventure I wi' see you tomorrow." A Jamaican might speak of an insect that "biteth like the serpent" or of a "righteous" court decision.

The idea behind
the Jamaican
proverb "If crab
nuh walk, him
don't grow claw"
is that "Travel
is the best
education."

JAMAICA-SPEAK

JAMAICAN	ENGLISH	JAMAICAN	ENGLISH
belly-god	glutton	Merica	America
bredda	brother	mi	me, I
brekfus	breakfast	mistress	married woman
chile	child	nyam	eat, food
dawta	daughter	ongle	only
deh	is, are	pickney	child
de	the	sinting	something
fah	for	teck	take
faisty	rude, impertinent	teef	steal
liad	liar	quashie	fool
mash	destroy	wakgud	goodbye
maskita	mosquito	(walk good)	

JAMAICAN	ENGLISH
"Everyt'ubf kool, mon? Everyt'ing irie?"	"Are you feeling good? Is everything alright?"
"Cuss-cuss never bore hole in skin."	"Words will never hurt me."
"If crab nuh walk, him don't grow claw."	"If a crab doesn't move around, it won't grow completely."

JAMAICAN ENGLISH

Jamaicans are educated in Standard English, which the popular daily newspaper *Jamaican Gleaner* also uses. In conversation, however, Jamaicans mix Standard English with colloquial words and expressions. The different language levels reflect Jamaica's social levels—the higher the level, the greater the use of Standard English.

Someone from a different culture may not understand every word of a casual conversation between two Jamaicans, but the general meaning is more or less discernible. Among friends and family, pronunciation, vocabulary, and grammar depart radically from Standard English. For example, "Di kuk di tel mi faamin, bot it nat so" means "The cook told me I was pretending, but it's not so." The main verb, "faamin," comes from the English word "form" but means "pretend."

When the slaves in Jamaica spoke English, they used grammatical structures that they were familiar with—those of African languages. For example, while Standard English expresses different noun relationships with different pronouns, Jamaican English may use one pronoun for different noun relationships. "I feel happy" becomes "Me happy," while "My book is lost" becomes "Me book lost."

What grammarians call "case" is also different in Jamaican English. Take "he," "him," and "his" as an example. The sentence "I kicked him" uses the objective case, because "him" is the object of the sentence. "I kicked his bag" uses the possessive case, because the bag belongs to someone. "He went home" uses the nominative case, because "he" is the subject of the sentence. In Jamaican English, all three examples use "him": "I kicked him," "I kicked him ball," and "Him went home."

In Jamaican English, the *dem* tag indicates a plural. For example, "de boy dem" means "the boys." One exception to this rule is the word "I," which is used twice to indicate "we." In dread talk, "I and I" conveys the Rastafarian sense that all people are equal.

Jamaican Creole grew out of a strong sense of the ridiculous and a gift for vivid imagery, earthy humor, and bawdy curses.

PRIDE IN THEIR LANGUAGE

Until recently, Jamaican English only existed in oral tradition, known as Jamaican Talk. It hardly ever appeared in print, and when it did it was usually ridiculed or condescendingly called "quaint." Yet it was the means of communication and expression for the majority of Jamaicans.

Before independence, there was social pressure to speak Standard English, which was seen as the norm. Any departure from Standard English was regarded as a deviation or an aberration. This unrealistic expectation fostered an inferiority complex in the majority of Jamaicans who could not speak Standard English. It was most damaging when Jamaicans had to deal with the British administration. In a court of law, for instance, Jamaicans were expected to speak as close to Standard English as possible. But as they struggled to communicate in a language they were uncomfortable with, the clarity of their presentation suffered as a result of nervousness and insecurity. Naturally, their case in court was weakened.

With independence and the growth of national consciousness came a new pride in Jamaican English. The reggae musician Bob Marley played a significant role in this process, because his international concert tours brought Jamaican English into prominence. His gift of expressing ideas and emotions in Jamaican English did enormous service to what was previously looked down on as "broken English." Jamaican Talk also found a place in dub poetry, or poetry in Jamaican English.

Academics have argued that Jamaican Creole should be recognized as a separate language. They point out that, historically, Jamaican Creole has evolved apart from English. Jamaican Creole is promoted for nationalistic and political motives as well. Some reason that Standard English is the language of a small elite and prevents the majority of Jamaican citizens from fully participating in their own society.

Jamaican Talk is characterized by irony, satire, and ridicule. The uninitiated may find it disconcerting at first but soon realize that the speakers aim their sarcasm at themselves as well.

THREE LANGUAGES?

Standard English will continue to be used in Jamaica because of its importance for international commerce. Abandoning English would isolate the island from the rest of the globe. At the same time, Jamaican Creole plays an important role in enabling Jamaicans to express their national and cultural identity with pride and a sense of history.

In addition, a Caribbean form of Standard English has developed. It represents a compromise between the two linguistic traditions and is gaining acceptance in schools and among employers.

Young people growing up in Jamaica use Jamaican Creole at home and Caribbean English in school and at work. Yet many aspire to be proficient in Standard English for success and prestige.

ARTS

BEFORE 1940 not much attention was paid to cultural self-expression through art in Jamaica. In the 1940s prominent Jamaican artists from every medium fueled a movement fostering national pride and the development of popular musical styles and a comprehensive network of museums, theaters, and galleries.

DANCE AND MUSIC

Jamaican dance, music, and song have a common origin in folktales and tradition. One of Jamaica's traditional dances is the mento. The name of the dance refers also to the accompanying music and lyrics. Mento musicians beat out the tune on bongo drums and the rhumba box, an instrument adapted from the African thumb piano. Mento singers recount tales of the past.

Above: **An artist touches up a painting at a handicraft market in Ocho Rios.**

Opposite: **A display of Jamaican wood carvings at a souvenir shop.**

The Jamaican quadrille started out as a folk dance brought to the island by Europeans. It was adapted by Jamaicans, who added African elements. Calypso, a jazz-influenced style of music, originated in Trinidad. It is especially popular in Jamaica's tourist areas, where it accompanies limbo dancers.

Jamaican work songs date back to when slaves made up songs to relieve boredom and hardship. The songs are short lyrical lines that are repeated. African influence can be detected in the alternation of lines between a lead singer and a chorus. But the work songs do not follow the call-and-response routine of African spirituals. They also differ from the traditional black spirituals of the southern United States; instead of soulful melancholy, there is optimism and a workaday atmosphere.

Bob Marley is credited with placing Jamaican music on the world stage. His house in Kingston is now a museum.

REGGAE

Jamaica's most distinctive and exciting music is reggae. It first emerged in the early 1970s, although its origins go back at least a decade before that, when Jamaican musicians created ska music, a blend of rhythm and blues and mento. The electric guitar and organ, which came from rhythm and blues, later became important instruments in reggae.

The origin of the word reggae is not clear. Perhaps it comes from the patois *streggae*, meaning rudeness or rude-boy, or *regge-regge*, meaning quarrel. It may also be a descriptive term, meaning regular, as the music has a regular, bass-dominated sound.

The lyrics of reggae music point to its street origins. Nearly all the early reggae musicians came from Kingston's slum areas, and their songs voiced the concerns of a dissatisfied African-Jamaican youth ignored by the established authorities. In the 1970s, Jamaican radio did not play reggae because of its political element. Bob Marley became reggae's superstar partly on talent and partly on his ethical stance toward political turmoil in Jamaica and toward the war in Vietnam.

Other big Jamaican reggae artists include Desmond Dekker, whose *Israelites* became Jamaica's first international hit, and Toots and the Maytals. Reggae also has a strong Rastafarian influence emphasizing peace, love, and reconciliation.

JIMMY CLIFF (1948–)

With the exception of Bob Marley, Jimmy Cliff is the best-known Jamaican singer and songwriter. His mix of traditional reggae with a soul element produces a very distinctive sound.

Cliff entered the music business with a song he wrote about a record store and an ice-cream parlor in Jamaica. One of the store's owners was so impressed by the song that he entered the record business and signed up Cliff. That was in 1962. Cliff was only 14 years old and living in near poverty. Two years later, he was touring the United States with such hits as *Hurricane Hattie* and *Miss Jamaica*. In 1969 his *Wonderful World, Beautiful People* became a big hit on both sides of the Atlantic.

In 1973 Cliff starred in the film *The Harder They*

Come, about a boy from the Jamaican countryside who goes to the capital to find work but falls into bad company. The film was an international success and introduced reggae to the world. It included a cross-section of some of the best reggae songs, such as Cliff's *Sitting in Limbo*, *Rivers of Babylon* by The Lemodians, and Desmond Dekker's *Shanty Town*.

Cliff continues to work internationally as a singer, producer, and actor. In 2003 he received the Order of Merit, which is given to a Jamaican citizen who has achieved eminent international distinction in science, arts, or literature. The award is the third highest honor in Jamaica, and no more than 15 living people can hold it.

BOB MARLEY (1945–81)

Bob Marley was born Robert Nesta Marley in the parish of Saint Ann to an Englishman, Norval Sinclair Marley, and an African-Jamaican woman, Cedella Malcom. When Marley was 12, he moved with his mother to the Trenchtown ghetto in Kingston.

When Marley was 17, he met Jimmy Cliff and produced his first song, *Judge Not*. Marley later signed with Island Records, which pioneered the marketing of full reggae albums and launched Marley to superstardom. Marley formed a band, The Wailing Wailers, and they started their own record label, Tuff Gong. In 1971 they had their first big hit, *Trenchtown Rock*, which stayed in the number-one position on the music charts in Jamaica for five months.

By then the band was known as The Wailers and began touring in Britain and the United States. Several of Marley's own compositions at that time were big hits by other artists, the best-known being *I Shot the Sheriff* by Eric Clapton and *Guava Jelly* by Barbra Streisand.

Despite the international success that The Wailers enjoyed, their roots remained in Jamaica and with Rastafarianism, and Marley, with all his fame and wealth, never forgot his ghetto roots. He returned to them in what is probably his most famous song, *No Woman, No Cry*, which was first released in 1975 and later covered by artists such as Boney M (1976) and The Fugees (1996). A verse of the song goes:

> "Said I remember when we used to sit,
> In the government yard in Trenchtown.
> And then Georgie would make the fire light,
> Log wood burnin' through the night.
> Then we would cook cornmeal porridge,
> Of which I'd share with you."

The political violence that rocked Jamaica in the 1970s saw an attempt on Marley's life in his own home in 1976. He recovered and continued his career, but in 1980 Marley collapsed on stage. He died eight months later from cancer. He was 36.

The Jamaican government organized a state funeral in Nine Miles, the village where Marley was born. Thousands attended the funeral, and the procession stretched for 55 miles (88 km). Shortly before his death, Marley had been awarded the Order of Merit.

LITERATURE

In 1949 Victor Stafford Reid's novel *New Day* marked the first attempt to explore what it meant to be Jamaican, as opposed to being a lost citizen of Africa or a European living in Jamaica. But more significantly, the novel was written in Jamaican dialect, and this opened the world of novels to the ordinary Jamaican.

The importance of the right language to reach Jamaican readers is reflected in the dedication a writer, Ken Maxwell, made in one of his books: "to all Jamaicans who have found that nowhere else in the world is real English spoken …" Jamaican English presents vivid impressions and moods that are instantly recognized by Jamaicans, and it gives them an empathy with the characters of a story in a way that Standard English often does not.

Other important Jamaican novelists include Roger Mais, Andrew Salkey, and Jamaica Kincaid. Mais and Salkey immigrated to Britain and never returned to live in Jamaica. Salkey wrote novels and children's stories, such as *Hurricane, Earthquake, Drought,* and *Riot.* Kincaid lives in the United States and is known for her moving renditions of growing up in Antigua. Some of her popular works are *Lucy* and *Mr. Potter.*

Mais only became a novelist in the last three years of his life. Born in 1905, he wrote only poetry and short stories until 1953, when his novel *The Hills Were Joyful Together* earned critical acclaim. The next year he published *Brother Man,* and in 1955, the year he died, *Black Lightning.* All three books are grim sociological studies of poverty and prison life, and are highly regarded.

Mais's books greatly influenced another gifted Jamaican writer, John Hearne. Hearne's novels, which include *Voices Under the Window* and *The Autumn Equinox,* have been described as sensitive and powerful.

Jamaican literature only emerged in the 20th century. Few Jamaicans were taught to read and write, and so literary works had a small audience.

99

Louise Bennett, the original dub poet, is known affectionately as Miss Lou.

DUB POETRY

Dub poetry has been called the baby of reggae. Although its emergence is associated with the 1970s, its roots can be found in the work of poet Louise Bennett. Since the early 1960s, Bennett has written poems in Jamaican English, ensuring that her audience, regardless of social class, can appreciate and enjoy her poems. Her poetry is firmly rooted in Jamaica's oral folk tradition, and she claims inspiration from the Bible and from Jamaican folk songs.

Bennett's poems first appeared in Jamaica's newspaper, but they are designed to be read aloud and turned into a performance. Her subject is life in modern Jamaica, covering topics such as public events, street life, and politics.

MICHAEL SMITH'S *MI CYAAN BELIEVE IT*

Mi seh mi cyaan believe it
Mi seh mi cyaan believe it
room dem a rent
mi apply within
but as me go in
cockroach rat an scorpion
    also come in

waan good
nose haffi run
but me naw go sideung
    pan igh wall
like Humpty Dumpty
mi a face me reality

In Standard English, *I Can't Believe It* might read:

I'm saying I can't believe it
I'm saying I can't believe it
rooms for rent
so I applied within
but as I went in
a cockroach, rat, and scorpion
    also came in

it wasn't good
I knew I had to run
but I can't go and sit
    upon the wall
like Humpty Dumpty
I have to face reality

When Bennett began writing poems, she was looked down on as someone who could only write in "broken English." When her first anthology appeared in 1966, a glossary of four pages was included to enable non-Jamaicans to understand her writing. Today she is a national figure, appreciated for her pioneering role in contemporary culture.

Bennett has inspired other dub poets, including Michael Smith, Mutabaruka, Linton Kwesi Johnson, and Oku Onora. Many of Jamaica's new dub poets had a university education and consciously turned away from Standard English to write in Jamaican English.

Johnson describes dub poetry in these terms: "Here the spoken/chanted word is the dominant mode. People's speech and popular music are combined with the Jamaican folk culture and the reggae tradition … as sources of inspiration and frames of reference."

A good example of dub poetry is Michael Smith's poem *Mi Cyaan Believe It* (*I Can't Believe It*). Like other dub poets, Smith composed his poems orally and then transcribed them.

Vibrant colors, tropical
landscapes, and African
animals are the main
features of Jamaican art.

ART

The oldest works of art in Jamaica, painted by the Taino Arawak on cave walls, are all the evidence that remains of the island's first inhabitants. Historians speculate that Arawak art influenced the Spanish artists who carved the friezes on the buildings of the first capital at St. Ann's Bay.

It was only well into the 20th century that non-European art began to receive any attention in Jamaica. Acknowledgment of the influence of African heritage on Jamaican art developed among the island's social elite. The sculptor Edna Manley, for example, focused on themes associated with the Jamaican consciousness.

Contemporary Jamaican popular art is drawn freely on the walls of buildings in Kingston's Tivoli Gardens area. The locality is considered a ghetto, but artistically it is rich in color and inspiration. It resembles a giant canvas where colors are splashed generously across the walls and yet integrated into a semiabstract theme. Pictorial subject matter often includes tropical landscapes and the flora and fauna of the island.

EDNA MANLEY (1900–)

Edna Manley is a talented sculptor whose wood carvings capture indigenous forms. They were seen as inferior and outrageous when they were first exhibited in 1936. But Manley was undaunted by criticism and continued to focus attention on Jamaican rather than imported values of aesthetic beauty.

Working with Robert Verity and the Institute of Jamaica in the 1940s, Manley was able to organize art lessons for young people at a price that they could afford. Eventually, that led to the establishment of the Jamaica School of Art in 1950.

Manley was a major influence on Jamaican art, being ideally placed to establish a liaison between politics and art. She was married to the late Norman Manley, who founded the People's National Party, and is the mother of the former prime minister, Michael Manley.

> *"The great thing was to be able to see ourselves as Jamaicans in Jamaica and try to free ourselves from the domination of English aesthetics."*
>
> *Edna Manley*

A number of self-taught artists have also attracted attention with their styles, which are similar to the styles of other intuitive artists working in different communities around the world. These painters have no unifying philosophy, and new styles keep emerging.

Some of the more famous painters in this group include Ralph Campbell, John Dunkley, and Mallica Reynolds. Reynolds, who paints under the pseudonym Kapo, is a Pocomanian, while the others are Rastafarians.

Jamaica's National Gallery houses the works of many of the island's most significant artists: landscapes by Ralph Campbell, realistic everyday scenes by David Pottinger, and abstract paintings by Eugene Hyde.

LEISURE

SPORTS ARE A POPULAR form of leisure in Jamaica, attracting both participants and spectators of all ages and social classes. Ball games, ranging from basketball and netball to cricket and football, are very popular, especially among younger Jamaicans. A large-scale sporting event such as an international cricket match attracts thousands of spectators, including picnicking families.

In a country blessed with beautiful beaches, spending a day at the beach is always a great way to relax with friends and family. Away from the beaches, dominoes is a popular game and, like chess, attracts dedicated players and watchers. Most Jamaican children play their first game of dominoes in school. There are special facilities for playing dominoes in most Jamaican community areas.

Left: **Cricket is a national sport in Jamaica.**

Opposite: **Jamaican girls play a street basketball game.**

STORYTELLING

Storytelling has always played an important role in Jamaican culture. During the 18th and 19th centuries, any overt demonstration of African heritage was forbidden, and in time only the remnants of traditional African activities such as games and dances survived.

Storytelling was an exception, because it could be carried on in the privacy of the slaves' dwellings. Stories from Africa were passed down from one generation to another. The most popular stories are those concerning Anansi, the spider man, and they often have a moral. A successful recital of an Anansi tale is theatrical in nature, and nuances of Jamaican patois are used to bring the story to life. Often, a story has key phrases repeated in a certain rhythm, adding drama to the story.

There are also stories about the days when men and women toiled for meager wages in the fields or on the waterfront weighing bananas and loading them onto the waiting boats.

With the advent of television, the art of storytelling is in danger of being lost. The poet Louise Bennett has worked to revive this leisure art form. She has traveled across Jamaica staging recitals and puppet shows to depict these traditional stories to Jamaica's youth today. The government has recognized the importance of the nation's oral tradition and encouraged its development.

ANANSI TALES

Anansi is cunning and witty, a survivor who is forced to live by his wits in order to cope with demanding circumstances. When luck is running his way he is a man, but when fate takes a turn for the worst and the future looks bleak, Anansi transforms into a spider and conceals himself in his web on the ceiling. A typical tale often ends with the words, "Jack mandora me no chose none," which means "I'm not responsible for the lies I've been telling."

The African origin of the Anansi tales is evident when Anansi encounters animals such as elephants and monkeys, which are not found in the Caribbean, but whose presence in a tale indicates its African origin.

FOLK SONGS

Work songs and church songs are two examples of how Jamaicans integrate their enjoyment of rhythm into daily life. Jamaica's folk songs, like other Jamaican music, are focused on rhythm.

One of the best loved Jamaican folk songs is *Day Dah Light* (*Day is Dawning*), also known as *Mr. Tallyman* or *Banana Boat Song*. Before Harry Belafonte made it popular in the 1960s, the song was sung by Jamaican women after a night on the wharf loading bananas on ships. The women carried heavy bunches of bananas on their heads. As they approached the ship, they called out to the tallyman who kept count of the bananas they carried by making notches on a piece of wood and splitting it in half so that each party got a record. The procession went on until daybreak when the women returned home to their children.

Jamaicans also like spirituals and revivalist songs, which reveal their belief in life after death and in the link between spirits and the living.

SOCCER

Soccer is a passion in Jamaica. Every year, high-school teams compete intensely for the Manning and DaCosta cups. National teams play at premier leagues organized by the Jamaica Football Federation.

Jamaican soccer has produced star players such as Lindy Delapenha, the first Jamaican to play in the English League, and in 1998 Jamaica's national team, the Reggae Boyz, reached the World Cup finals in France.

The West Indies at the Oval stadium in 1939. Jamaica's cricket legend George Headley reaches to hit a ball from the English cricket team.

CRICKET

The English introduced cricket to Jamaica in the mid-19th century. The game was initially strongly associated with the English upper classes but soon caught on with all sections of Jamaican society. For a long time, however, national teams were sometimes chosen along social or racial lines. It was not until the 1960s that racial prejudice ceased to influence the selection of teams.

The prestigious international cricket games, or test matches, involve eight teams: the West Indies, England, Australia, New Zealand, India, Pakistan, Sri Lanka, and South Africa. One test match is played for five days, sometimes with a rest day between the third and fourth days.

Jamaica invariably has a strong presence on the West Indies team. Business comes almost to a halt in Jamaica when a test match is played. The 12,000 seats at the main cricket ground are sold out, and every radio

JAMAICA'S GREATEST CRICKETERS

During the 1970s, the West Indies team was the clear favorite for every test match it played. That would not have been the case without Michael Holding (*right*), a Jamaican.

For years Holding was the world's fastest cricket bowler, and his ability to spin the ball so that it rose toward the batsman's face was a test of nerves for any batsman.

Another all-time great was George Alphonso Headley. He was born in Panama to a Jamaican mother who brought him up in Jamaica.

Headley began to play cricket in the early 1920s. He holds the distinction of being the only player to score 200 runs at Lords in London, the Yankee Stadium of international cricket.

A fast-paced bowler can send the ball hurtling toward the batsman at a speed of more than 90 miles (145 km) an hour.

and television station broadcasts the game live. The atmosphere resembles a combination of Thanksgiving and the Superbowl in the United States. Victory for the West Indies team is an immediate occasion for national celebration in Jamaica.

Jamaican cricketers are renowned for their bowling and batting, and their fast bowling has particularly caught the imagination of cricket enthusiasts the world over. In addition to speed, the bowler's skill is measured by his ability to vary his technique so that the batsman is continually surprised. A "googly," for instance, is a ball spun in a counterclockwise motion so that it spins away from the batsman after it bounces, which makes it more difficult to hit. The "off-cutter," on the other hand, spins toward the batsman, and if the batsman is not prepared for it, there is a danger that he will miss the ball and have his wicket broken.

THE PITCH Cricket matches are played in a stadium with a central rectangular pitch 22 yards (20 m) long. At each end of the pitch, there is a wicket, a wooden frame made of three vertical 2.5-foot (75-cm) stumps and two horizontal crosspieces on top.

THE PLAYERS Two teams of eleven players a side take turns to bat. The object of the batting side is to score runs. The object of the bowling side is to dismiss the batsmen. The game is divided into innings; each inning ends when 10 batsmen have been dismissed.

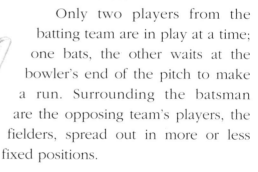

Only two players from the batting team are in play at a time; one bats, the other waits at the bowler's end of the pitch to make a run. Surrounding the batsman are the opposing team's players, the fielders, spread out in more or less fixed positions.

SCORING RUNS The batsman tries to strike the ball past or over the fielders so that while the opposing team is retrieving the ball, he and his team player can score runs. To score a run, they have to run the distance between the two wickets.

If the batsman strikes the ball well enough, he and his partner may score a number of runs. The opposing team will try to get him "out" by breaking

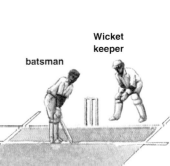

Wicket keeper

batsman

the wicket while they are in mid-run. That is called being "run out." The batsman has to avoid being caught out, and the safest shots are those played along the ground.

Keeping score requires concentration, because there are many ways to score. For example, if the ball is hit high enough to reach the boundary of the playing area without touching the ground, the batsman automatically scores six runs; if it reaches the boundary area along the ground, four runs are scored.

22 yards

bowler

batsman's team player

Every batsman aspires to reach 100 runs, or a "century." Every batsman's night-mare is being dismissed with-out scoring a single run, or being "bowled for a duck."

umpire

THE WICKET The batsman has the task of defending his wicket with his bat, while the bowler attempts to break the wicket with each delivery of the ball.

If the bowler is successful, the batsman is "bowled out," and another player on his team takes over. If a bowler takes three wickets with successive deliveries of the ball, he is said to have taken a "hat-trick."

There are many strokes that can be played by the batsman, from the forward defensive shot to the attacking cover drive or hook shot.

FESTIVALS

JAMAICA HAS 10 national holidays. The religious holidays include Christmas, Ash Wednesday, Good Friday, and Easter Monday. The nonreligious holidays are New Year's Day, Labor Day, Emancipation Day, National Heroes Day, and Independence Day. Other celebrations that Jamaicans look forward to every year include national beauty pageants and Carnival.

INDEPENDENCE DAY AND "FESTIVAL!"

The major festival that brings all Jamaicans together in a spirit of celebration is Independence Day. The first Monday in August is the day scheduled for the major events, which are the culmination of various events and activities in the preceding weeks. The months of July and August are celebrated under the banner of Festival.

Events include competitions in different areas of the arts, such as painting, sculpture, song, dance, and drama. Participants come from schools, churches, and other community organizations, or they may be professionals in the arts. The winners of the costume competition are crowned "king" and "queen."

In addition, an agricultural show in Denbigh, May Pen, educates and entertains with displays of the livestock and skills of farmers from the various parishes. On Independence Day itself, floats, marching bands, and costumed dancers parade in the streets of Kingston toward the national stadium for main celebrations.

Preparations for Independence Day celebrations begin early in the year. Young Jamaicans are encouraged to participate in one way or another through their schools. Working behind the scenes to organize the grand, elaborate shows and displays that the islanders and tourists enjoy every year, young Jamaicans learn about their cultural heritage.

Opposite: **A guitar and banjo, maracas, and their voices are all it takes a band of Jamaican musicians to generate a festive atmosphere.**

Jamaicans have won the Miss World title three times: Carole Joan Crawford in 1963, Cindy Breakspeare in 1976, and Lisa Hanna in 1993.

CARNIVAL

Jamaicans celebrated their first Carnival event in 1991, thanks to the musician Byron Lee, who worked with supporters to organize what was to become Jamaica's biggest festival.

Similar to Carnival celebrations in other countries, the Jamaica Carnival has music, dancing, costumes, parades, and general merrymaking. One difference, however, is that the Jamaica Carnival is celebrated through Easter rather than before Lent.

For Jamaicans, the Carnival is not just a big music and dance festival. It unites Jamaicans from different social classes and walks of life. During Carnival celebrations, people take to the streets in the hundreds of thousands to party and celebrate life together, ignoring cultural and social barriers. Many also watch the celebrations on television.

The Jamaica Carnival is an outlet for the talents of the island's own musicians and fashion designers, who make the music and create the costumes that color the festival in Kingston and other cities such as Montego Bay and Negril.

CHRISTMAS

Jamaicans start preparing for Christmas as early as mid-November, when by tradition grandmothers put dried fruit in strong white rum to soak. In December, the fruit is poured into cake batter, and brown sugar and molasses are added. The cakes are baked and stored for Christmas.

Another traditional practice at Christmas involves the making and drinking of sorrel, a garnet-colored sweet wine with a spicy flavor that comes from ginger and pimento seeds. Both sorrel and fruit cake may be stored away to "mature," sometimes for years, but the cakes must be periodically seasoned with liquor.

Older Jamaicans remember the days when whole families set out on Christmas Eve for the long walk to a market town to sell their farm produce at the Grand Market. They bought tins of wet sugar, which they flavored with ginger and nutmeg and left to harden in banana leaves to make a children's Christmas treat called sugar head. They also bought special chocolates made from dried cocoa pods to grate into hot milk and sweeten to make a drink called chocolate tea.

Jamaicans enjoy special treats at Christmastime.

Unlike in the United States, in Jamaica cards and gifts are not a Christmas custom. One of the main reasons is poverty. Another reason is that most Jamaicans see Christmas as primarily a religious event.

MISS JAMAICA

There are two major beauty pageants in Jamaica every year. The Miss Jamaica World and Miss Jamaica Universe competitions generate great excitement across the island, because the winner goes on to represent the country in the Miss World and Miss Universe competitions. The winners of the international competitions will enjoy fame, fortune, and the chance to promote an environmental or humanitarian cause. Since 1963 three Jamaican women have won the coveted Miss World title—an extraordinary achievement for a relatively small population.

NATIONAL HEROES DAY

On the third Monday in October, Jamaicans get a day away from work and school to remember seven remarkable individuals who dedicated their lives to the cause of bringing about greater freedom and equality in Jamaican society.

The six men and one woman were awarded the Order of National Hero, the highest honor in the country, in recognition of their contribution to the social development of Jamaica.

The only woman among the seven, known as Nanny, led the Maroons in guerrilla warfare against colonialists during the first Maroon War, between 1720 and 1739. It was said that Nanny could catch the enemy's musket balls and fire them back.

Sam Sharpe (1801–32) was declared a national hero posthumously (*above, a statue of Sharpe*) for his role in leading the slave rebellion that began the fight for the end of the slave trade.

George William Gordon (1820–65) is also remembered for his role in the fight against slavery. His mother was a slave and his father a planter. Gordon championed a movement in the mid-1880s that sought political rights for freed slaves.

Paul Bogle (1822–65) campaigned against injustice and poverty and participated in the slave rebellion of 1865 that led to his execution.

The remaining national heroes lived in the 20th century. Marcus Garvey (1887–1940) and Alexander Bustamante (1884–1977) represented and campaigned for the rights of working-class Jamaicans, while Norman Manley (1893–1969) is honored as the founder of the People's National Party and the leader who negotiated Jamaica's independence from Britain.

LABOR DAY

Jamaicans celebrate Labor Day on May 23. The day is dedicated to Sam Sharpe, who instigated a rebellion of slaves in 1831, thus starting the movement toward the abolition of slavery. On May 23, 1832, Sharpe was hanged in the Montego Bay square, which was later named after him. Around 500 of his fellow rebels were also executed.

REGGAE FESTIVALS

Jamaicans celebrate several reggae festivals annually in different cities around the island. Two of the biggest festivals are the Reggae Sumfest, previously called Sunsplash, in Montego Bay and the Reggae Superjam in Kingston.

REGGAE SUMFEST Started in 1978, this week-long festival takes place in Montego Bay in the second half of the month of July. The festival features top local and international reggae musicians, such as Ziggy Marley and The Melody Makers, Byron Lee and The Dragonaires, Sean Paul, Shaggy, Beyoncé, D'Angelo, and Maxi Priest. One of the most memorable Reggae Sumfest events took place in 1981, when Stevie Wonder came from the United States to pay tribute to the recently deceased Bob Marley.

Crowds turn up for the Reggae Sumfest each year to catch the acts performing on stage or on the beach. The line-up each night starts late in the evening and goes on until early in the morning.

REGGAE SUPERJAM Held on December 28 in Kingston, the Reggae Superjam concert has featured some of Jamaica's best reggae acts, including in 1983 the legendary Peter Tosh.

The pantomime involves elaborate costumes.

PANTOMIME

A pantomime is traditionally a dramatic performance in which a story is told through expressive body and facial movements. It is usually based on an English fairytale and performed around Christmas.

Introduced to Jamaica by the British, the pantomime has evolved and encouraged the development of local writers, directors, and performers. Today, Jamaica has a pantomime festival in Kingston.

Like the English pantomime, the Jamaican pantomime is performed around Christmas and has the set characters of the Dame, a hero, and a heroine.

Unlike the English pantomime, Jamaica's pantomime includes other characters, such as Anansi the spider man, and the rhythms of the English music-hall and folk songs have been replaced by Pocomanian drum beats and the movements of the John Canoe dances.

The Jamaican pantomime has no special association with fairytales, preferring instead stories such as *The Pirate Princess*, based on the real-life events of two women pirates who sailed with Calico Jack in the 17th century, or dramatic satires of government policies and politicians. The audience is also expected to participate by throwing in their own humorous contributions.

THE TRADITION OF JOHN CANOE

The tradition of John Canoe may have originated in the 1600s with bands of strolling players performing in the streets for money and food.

In the weeks leading up to the Grand Market Day on Christmas Eve, John Canoe dancers practice late into the night to coordinate precisely the mixing of drum music and dance. The performance is a combination of African dance and European masquerade, and the dancers accept small donations from spectators to help cover costs, but they are not professionals and their aim is not to make a profit.

John Canoe dancers are dressed in elaborate animal costumes. The dancer who takes the part of John Canoe himself wears a costume that

includes symbolic head gear incorporating the tusks of a boar. He always carries a sword, trails the tail of a cow, and leads the procession by a display of his acrobatic skills.

His players follow, dressed to resemble characters from an elite European court, including a king and a queen. Over the years, the procession has become an occasion for players to dress in the spirit of a carnival that has little connection to the original John Canoe dance. For example, there may be a mock police officer pretending to keep the group in order, an actor dressed as a pregnant woman dancing along, and a few dancers dressed as Arawak Indians joining in for good measure.

The John Canoe tradition, sometimes called Jonkonnu, is associated with Christmas because, in the 17th century, that was the only time of the year that the slaves had a holiday. The word Jonkonnu, meaning sorcerer of death, may have come from secret societies in West Africa. That may explain the rule that dancers and musicians must communicate with one another by whispering during the procession.

FOOD

THE TYPICAL JAMAICAN DIET is based on locally grown foods such as yams, bananas, breadfruit, sweet potatoes, pineapples, and coconuts, although supermarkets in the capital display many food products familiar to North American families.

The typical Jamaican kitchen, especially in rural areas, does not depend on electricity but on fuels such as gas, paraffin, or wood. Open-back trucks loaded with gas cylinders are a common sight in towns and villages. Paraffin stoves are also common. Wood fires are used both inside and outside the home. Barbecuing on an outdoor wood fire is a way of saving on the cost of fuels such as gas. In the larger towns, electricity is more popular among families who can afford to invest in an electric stove.

Minimal basic utensils are found in most Jamaican kitchens. The average home is equipped with two pots, or kerosene tins adapted to function as pots. The large, durable leaves of the banana plant may serve as plates, a custom that the early Indian laborers were familiar with.

Above: **Jamaica's congenial weather provides a variety of tropical fruit and vegetables throughout the year.**

Opposite: **A fresh fruit and sugarcane seller in Montego Bay.**

FOOD HERITAGE

Jamaican food has a distinctive genealogy. It has evolved as a mixture of African, European, Chinese, and Indian cuisines. The slaves brought with them their traditional style of cooking and methods of curing and preserving food. The laborers who came later from China and India also brought their cooking styles—light stir-frying, and slow-cooking for curries such as curried goat, a standard dish at celebrations.

Ripe ackees, a famous Jamaican fruit, are poisonous before they ripen and open. The creamy flesh is then cooked with salted fish in a dish unique to Jamaica.

TRADITIONAL INGREDIENTS Long before the Europeans arrived in Jamaica, the Taino Arawak cultivated sweet potatoes, pineapples, and coconuts. Jamaican cuisine still uses these ingredients. Coconuts, for example, are readily available and inexpensive and are used in various ways: to make cold pudding, fudge, or sauce.

The pimento tree is native to Jamaica, where it grows wild on the limestone hills. Dried pimento berries yield a spice that combines the flavors of clove, nutmeg, and cinnamon. Pimento has thus earned the name allspice. Jamaica is the world's largest supplier of pimento, which is used in many recipes.

The ackee tree was introduced to Jamaica from West Africa toward the end of the 18th century. Its leathery leaves, more than 20 feet (6 m) in height, are a bright orange-red. Inside the poisonous 3-inch (7.6-cm) fruit are black seeds containing an edible yellow flesh.

Rice, Asian spices, and vegetables from the Orient were introduced to Jamaica by Chinese and Indian laborers.

FAVORITE DISHES

Sunday lunch is a special family event. The main dish is usually roast beef or chicken. While roast beef betrays an English influence, it is served with rice rather than potatoes. Rice owes its place on the Jamaican table to the Chinese influence. Typical vegetables that accompany a meal include yams, sweet potatoes, pumpkin, and peas.

THE NATIONAL DISH "Ackee and sal'fish," or ackee and salted fish, has been eaten at home for as long as Jamaicans can remember, but it is relatively new on tourist menus, where it is included under "authentic Jamaican cuisine."

Jerked chicken and pork. Jamaican jerked meat has a smoky taste.

The kidney-shaped yellow flesh that is removed from the center of the ackee seed has a nutty flavor when cooked. "Ackee and sal'fish" is a small dish, but for a more substantial meal it can be served with fried plantain, boiled green bananas, or lightly fried flour dumplings called johnny cakes.

JERKED PORK Another popular roadside dish is pork that is spiced and cooked over an open fire. Jerked pork was once a Maroon speciality cooked over a fire of green pimento wood. Today, that style of cooking is also used for other meats, such as chicken. Jerked meat stalls are a common sight along the roads in Jamaica.

Breadfruit is a staple food in Jamaica. The breadfruit tree grows very tall, but some of the branches hang low enough for a child to reach and pick the fruit.

OTHER FAVORITES Apart from "ackee and sal'fish," other Jamaican seafood favorites include peppered shrimp, stuffed crayfish, and red snapper, all eaten with rice and slices of onion, peppers, and tomatoes. Some small roadside cafés specialize in seafood seasoned with pepper and roasted on zinc sheets over a wood fire.

Another popular dish is a vegetarian stew of rice, peas, red beans, and coconut milk. Its special taste is enhanced with onions and pepper. Pig's tail or salted beef may be added.

Fresh fruit is available throughout the year, and local varieties provide a lot of choice for dessert. Papayas or pawpaws, naseberries, pineapples, or bananas in coconut sauce provide a typical end to a meal.

SOME UNIQUELY JAMAICAN FOODS

The names of some Jamaican foods are not commonly found in North America or Europe. Some of the more interesting ones are:

BREADFRUIT A large, green fruit about 8 inches (20 cm) in diameter, breadfruit can be roasted, fried, or boiled. It features regularly in the Jamaican diet because of its 30- to 40-percent carbohydrate content.

Breadfruit was introduced to the Caribbean from Tahiti in 1793 by Captain William Bligh on his second attempt. His earlier attempt, in 1787, led to the famous mutiny by his crew, depicted in the novel and film *Mutiny on the Bounty.* To ensure that there was enough water for the breadfruit seedlings, the captain denied the crew drinking water. The crew set the captain adrift in a small boat and threw the breadfruit overboard.

MATRIMONY A dessert consisting of segments of orange covered with mashed star apple in cream.

NASEBERRY Also called sapodilla, this small fruit has rough, brown skin and a soft, sweet flesh.

ORTANIQUE This citrus fruit (*right*) is a hybrid of orange and tangerine. The name ortanique combines the words orange, tangerine, and unique. Jamaica cultivates ortanique for local consumption and for export.

RUNDOWN This traditional main dish consists of cod or mackerel simmered in coconut milk and then mixed with onions and pepper.

STAMP AND GO This is the local name for quick-fried, bite-size pieces of salted fish. Stamp and go is often available at roadside food stalls.

RECIPE FOR CURRIED GOAT MEAT

This recipe serves six.

2 large onions, sliced
5 pounds (2¼ kg) young goat meat, cubed
Oil or vegetable shortening
2 tablespoons curry powder
1 red pepper, sliced
Bay leaf

½ teaspoon allspice
Salt and pepper
1 cup beef or chicken stock
1 cup coconut milk
Juice of 1 lime

Sauté the onions, and brown the meat in the oil or shortening. Add the curry powder and red pepper. Stir over medium heat for 3 minutes. Add the bay leaf, allspice, salt, pepper, and stock, and simmer for at least two hours. Add the coconut milk, and simmer for another 30 minutes. Add the lime juice just before serving.

RECIPE FOR PLANTAIN FRITTERS

4½ tablespoons self-rising flour
6 tablespoons plain flour
½ cup water
¾ teaspoon sugar

Oil for deep-frying
2 plantains, each peeled and sliced into 4 pieces
Juice of 1 lime

Sift all the flour into a bowl. Add the water, and stir to form a smooth, thick batter. Add the sugar, and stir well. Heat the oil in a deep pan until smoking hot. Coat the plantains with the batter, and slide into the oil. Fry for 5 minutes until golden brown. Serve with the lime juice.

DRINKS

Popular Jamaican drinks are made using coconut water and goat's milk. The variety of fruit on the island provides opportunities to create many flavors by mixing the juice of different fruits. One popular beverage is made by mixing tamarind juice, soursop, and coconut water.

First brewed by the Arabs of Yemen from the seeds of a small evergreen tree, coffee was introduced to Jamaica in 1728. One type of coffee grown in Jamaica is reputed to have such exceptional taste that it commands the highest price of any brand of coffee in the world. It is named after the Blue Mountains.

Alcohol plays a significant role in Jamaican culture. Bars are found everywhere and provide a central focus for socializing. No one type of alcoholic drink is especially popular, although cold beer is ubiquitous. The local brand Red Stripe, which is produced by the company that sponsors the Reggae Sumfest, got the nickname "The Policeman" from the red stripe on the pants of the Jamaican police uniform.

The more expensive alcoholic drinks are the liqueurs, some of which, such as Tía María, have become standard items in bars and liquor stores around the world.

Jamaica's most famous drink is rum, often blended with different fruits to produce unique fruit liquors. Rum is also widely used in fruit punches, the most popular being planter's punch, a blend of lime juice, syrup, and rum, flavored with angostura bitters and cooled with a lot of crushed ice.

Most Jamaican cooking ingredients are found in the community markets. This one is in Savanna la Mar in western Jamaica.

Inside a rum distillery.

RUM

Rum is a spirit distilled from freshly crushed sugarcane or from the fermentation of molasses, a by-product of the sugarcane industry. Rum has a long history in Jamaica. The slaves were encouraged to make it, and the drink was readily available to everyone working on sugar plantations. It was used to pacify the laborers and help them deal with their discontent away from their homeland.

When Jamaica was wrested from the Spaniards by the English, rum was introduced to England for the first time. It enjoyed a big boost in popularity when the British navy decided, for the same motives as the plantation owners, to dispense a free amount of the drink to all sailors.

Rum is distilled wherever sugarcane is grown, but Jamaican rum is the most famous. What gives rum its unique quality is the presence of sugar from the start of distillation. Other spirits such as whisky and gin depend on an initial stage of malting when starch is converted to sugar. Because the distillation of rum does not require that stage, it is purer and retains the original flavor.

JAMAICAN RUM

What gives Jamaican rum its special status is in the distillation process. Each distillery has a unique process of adding flavors and blending, and this makes one brand of rum different from another.

The most famous brand of rum in Jamaica is Appleton, made by Wray and Nephew in Kingston, although its sugar estates are in the southwest of the island.

Rums of different ages, depending on how many years they have been left to mature in their casks, are blended together to produce the special Appleton taste. The wooden casks must be kept as cool as possible to minimize any loss through evaporation. The warehouses have special roofs that allow water to run over them constantly and keep the temperature down to an acceptable level. A distillery such as that of Wray and Nephew keeps the details of its actual blending process a secret to maintain the exclusivity of its brand.

Prestigious Jamaican rums may be stored for up to 15 years before they are made available for sale and export. Appleton Special rum is sold in more than 800 cities around the world. When former U.S. President Ronald Reagan visited Jamaica, he was presented with a case of Appleton rum that was more than 100 years old.

Jamaicans drink different types of rum. For many, their favorite rum will be one distilled according to a traditional recipe and made only for local consumption, most likely a white rum in a very pure form—100 proof, according to the measure of the purity of alcohol.

The international brands of rum have been adulterated so that their proof is reduced. Adulterating rum adds to the cost of the final drink, which is another reason why pure white rum is inexpensive and more popular. Practitioners of traditional medicine use the cheap white rum as a rubbing lotion for backache. Ganja soaked in white rum and smoked is highly regarded as a general cure-all for minor medical complaints.

JAMAICAN RICE AND BEANS

This recipe makes 8 to 12 servings.

1 cup dried kidney beans
4 cups coconut milk
1 clove garlic
½ teaspoon dried thyme
3 cups uncooked rice (preferably basmati)
2½ cups water
2 teaspoons salt
1 teaspoon sugar

Soak the kidney beans overnight. Combine with the coconut milk in a saucepan. Cover and cook about one hour, until the beans are tender but not mushy. Add the remaining ingredients. Cover and cook about 15 minutes over medium heat until the rice absorbs all the liquid.

JAMAICAN PUMPKIN SOUP

This recipe makes 6 servings.

2 tablespoons butter or margarine
2 finely chopped large onions
2 pounds pumpkin, peeled and cut in chunks
4 cups chicken stock
1 cup light cream
salt and pepper to taste

Melt the butter or margarine in a saucepan. Fry the onions until transparent. Add the pumpkin and chicken stock, and simmer until the pumpkin softens. Leave to cool. Mix in a blender for a few seconds. Return the mixture to the saucepan. Add the cream, salt, and pepper. Simmer for five minutes. Serve hot.

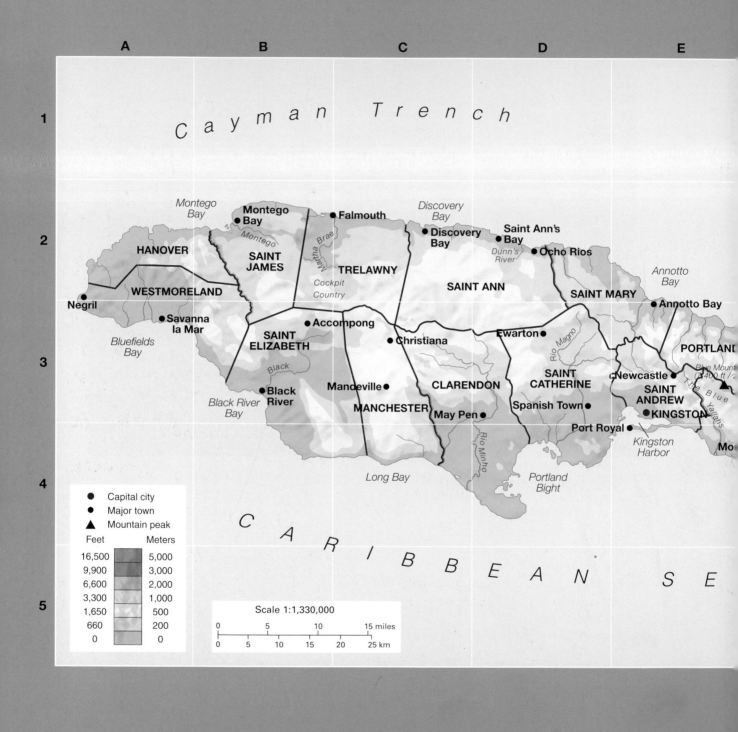

A
B
C
D
E

1

Cayman Trench

2

Montego Bay

Montego Bay

● **Falmouth**

Discovery Bay

Saint Ann's Bay

HANOVER

SAINT JAMES

Montego

Martha Brae

TRELAWNY

● **Discovery Bay**

● **Ocho Rios**

Dunn's River

Annotto Bay

WESTMORELAND

Cockpit Country

SAINT ANN

SAINT MARY

● **Negril**

Bluefields Bay

● **Savanna la Mar**

● **Accompong**

Black

SAINT ELIZABETH

● **Christiana**

● **Ewarton**

Rio Magno

● **Annotto Bay**

PORTLAND

3

Black River Bay

● **Black River**

● **Mandeville**

CLARENDON

MANCHESTER

● **May Pen**

SAINT CATHERINE

● **Spanish Town**

● **Newcastle**

Blue Mount (5400 ft /

SAINT ANDREW

● **KINGSTON**

▲

The Blue

Yallahs

● **Port Royal**

Kingston Harbor

Mo

4

Long Bay

Rio Minho

Portland Bight

_C A R I B B E A N S E_

5

●	Capital city
●	Major town
▲	Mountain peak

Feet		Meters
16,500		5,000
9,900		3,000
6,600		2,000
3,300		1,000
1,650		500
660		200
0		0

Scale 1:1,330,000

0   5   10   15 miles

0   5   10   15   20   25 km

MAP OF JAMAICA

ECONOMIC JAMAICA

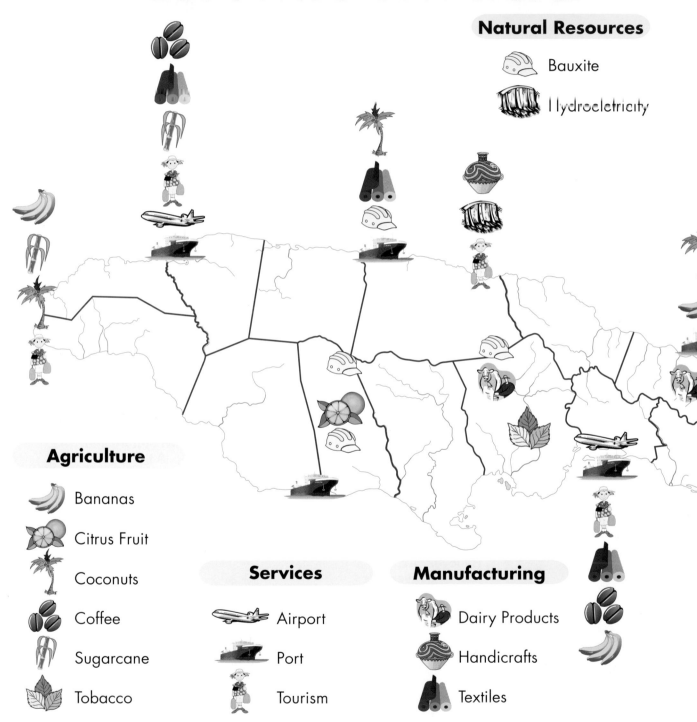

Natural Resources

Bauxite

Hydroelctricity

Agriculture

Bananas

Citrus Fruit

Coconuts

Coffee

Sugarcane

Tobacco

Services

Airport

Port

Tourism

Manufacturing

Dairy Products

Handicrafts

Textiles

ABOUT
THE ECONOMY

ECONOMIC OVERVIEW
Still recovering from the recession in the mid-1990s, the Jamaican economy suffers from high interest rates, stiff foreign competition, and a poor exchange rate. Jamaica's economic future rests on the growth of tourism and foreign investment and on improvements in economic policy and the exchange rate.

GROSS DOMESTIC PRODUCT (GDP)
$9.7 billion

GDP SECTORS
Services 63 percent, industry 31 percent, agriculture 6 percent (2002 est.)

LAND AREA
4,182 square miles (10,831 square km)

NATURAL RESOURCES
Bauxite, gypsum, limestone

AGRICULTURAL PRODUCTS
Bananas, citrus fruit, coffee, potatoes, poultry, sugarcane, vegetables

CURRENCY
1 Jamaican dollar (JMD) = 100 cents
Notes: 10, 20, 50, 100, 500 dollars
Coins: 1, 10, 25 cents; 1, 5, 10 dollars
USD 1 = JMD 60.25 (April 2004)

INDUSTRIAL PRODUCTS
Bauxite, cement, metals, paper, textiles

WORKFORCE
1.11 million

INTERNATIONAL AIRPORTS
Norman Manley (Kingston), Sangster (Montego Bay)

PORTS AND HARBORS
Discovery Bay, Kingston, Montego Bay, Ocho Rios, Port Antonio

MAJOR EXPORTS
Alumina, bananas, bauxite, chemicals, clothing, rum, sugar

MAJOR IMPORTS
Chemicals, construction materials, fertilizer, fuel, machinery, transportation equipment

TRADE PARTNERS
Canada, Germany, Japan, the Netherlands, Norway, Trinidad and Tobago, the United Kingdom, the United States

UNEMPLOYMENT RATE
15.4 percent (2002 est.)

INFLATION RATE
7 percent (2002 est.)

EXTERNAL DEBT
$5.3 billion (2002)

CULTURAL JAMAICA

Sam Sharpe Square
Sam Sharpe Square in the heart of Montego Bay features bronze statues of the national hero Sharpe preaching to his followers. Montego Bay also boasts one of Jamaica's best handicrafts markets.

Cockpit Country
Visitors can ride a helicopter for an awesome view of this limestone plateau or walk a difficult trail through the virtually untouched terrain.

Columbus Park
The park provides wide views of Discovery Bay, the site of Christopher Columbus' landing in 1494. Buildings from the Spanish colonial period still stand in the park.

Dunn's River Falls
Shaded by the forest canopy, the falls in Ocho Rios provide a cool walk along limestone steps that lead down to Turtle Beach. The falls' waters are tapped for hydroelectricity.

Port Antonio
This quiet port was in the late 19th and early 20th century the banana capital of the world. Its tropical beauty has attracted celebrities since Errol Flynn fell so in love with the town that he bought an island there.

Seven-mile Beach
The most popular vacation spot in Negril, 7 miles (11 km) of beautiful beach, is a sun lover's dream. The city also has Jamaica's first conservation area, which protects marine and mangrove life.

Mandeville
The center of the island's bauxite industry offers tours to bauxite mines as well as boat or fishing tours and tours to coffee and chocolate factories.

Old Capital
The island capital from the early 16th to the late 19th century, Spanish Town showcases many buildings from the periods of Spanish and English occupation. An iron bridge leading into the old capital dates back to 1801.

Bob Marley Museum
Tourists visit the late reggae star's home in Kingston to see the tree under which he practiced playing his guitar. Kingston also attracts with a handicrafts market and a national art gallery.

Morant Bay Fort
The fort and courthouse at Morant Bay were the site of the 1865 rebellion led by Paul Bogle, who died for the cause of freedom and was declared a national hero. His statue stands in front of the courthouse.

ABOUT THE CULTURE

COUNTRY NAME
Jamaica

CAPITAL
Kingston

OTHER MAJOR CITIES
Montego Bay, Negril, Ocho Rios, Port Antonio, Port Royal

PARISHES
Clarendon, Hanover, Manchester, Portland, Saint Andrew, Saint Ann, Saint Catherine, Saint Elizabeth, Saint James, Saint Mary, Saint Thomas, Trelawney, Westmoreland

NATIONAL FLAG
A gold diagonal cross with black triangles on the sides and green triangles at the top and bottom

NATIONAL ANTHEM
Jamaica, Land We Love. Adopted in 1962. Words by Hugh Braham Sherlock. Music by Robert Charles Lightbourne. To listen, visit www.jamaicans.com /info/anth.htm

POPULATION
About 2.7 million (2003 est.)

LANGUAGES
English (official), Jamaican Creole (patois)

ETHNIC GROUPS
African 90.9 percent; African-European 7.3 percent; East Indian 1.3 percent; other 1.4 percent

RELIGIOUS GROUPS
Christian (Protestant 61.3 percent, Roman Catholic 4 percent); Rastafarian, animist, other 34.7 percent

IMPORTANT ANNIVERSARIES
Labor Day (May 23), Emancipation Day (August 1), Independence Day (August 6), National Heroes Day (third Monday in October)

LEADERS IN POLITICS
Alexander Bustamante (prime minister 1962–67), Norman Manley (People's National Party founder), Edward Seaga (prime minister 1980–89), Michael Manley (prime minister 1972–80, 1989–92), Percival James Patterson (prime minister since 1993)

LEADERS IN THE ARTS
Louise Bennett (poet and folklorist), Jimmy Cliff (singer and songwriter), Linton Kwesi Johnson (poet and musician), Roger Mais (novelist), Edna Manley (sculptor), Robert Nesta Marley (musician and songwriter), Victor Stafford Reid (novelist)

NATIONAL BIRD
Streamer-tailed hummingbird, a.k.a. Doctor Bird

NATIONAL FLOWER
Lignum vitae

NATIONAL FOOD
Ackee and saltfish

TIME LINE

IN JAMAICA	IN THE WORLD
	753 B.C. Rome is founded.
	116–17 B.C. The Roman Empire reaches its greatest extent, under Emperor Trajan (98–17).
A.D. 600–700 Taino Arawak arrive from Venezuela and the Guyanas.	**A.D. 600** Height of Mayan civilization
1494 The Spanish arrive.	**1000** The Chinese perfect gunpowder and begin to use it in warfare.
1515 The Taino Arawak all but disappear; the first slaves are brought from Africa.	**1530** Beginning of trans-Atlantic slave trade organized by the Portuguese in Africa.
	1558–1603 Reign of Elizabeth I of England
	1620 Pilgrims sail the *Mayflower* to America.
1640 Sugarcane is introduced as a major crop.	
1655 The British invade.	
1692 An earthquake strikes Port Royal.	
1739 Signing of the Maroon peace treaty	**1776** U.S. Declaration of Independence
	1789–1799 The French Revolution
1832 Sam Sharpe, leader of the great slave rebellion, is hanged in Montego Bay.	
1838 Slavery is completely abolished; indentured servants arrive from Europe and Asia.	**1861** The U.S. Civil War begins.
1865 The Morant Bay rebellion; Paul Bogle and George William Gordon are executed.	**1869** The Suez Canal is opened.

IN JAMAICA	IN THE WORLD
1866	
Jamaica becomes a Crown colony.	
1872	
Kingston becomes the new capital.	
1907	
An earthquake destroys most of Kingston.	**1914**
	World War I begins.
	1939
1944	World War II begins.
All adults are granted the right to vote.	**1945**
	The United States drops atomic bombs on Hiroshima and Nagasaki.
	1949
	The North Atlantic Treaty Organization (NATO) is formed.
	1957
1962	The Russians launch Sputnik.
Jamaica gains independence.	**1966-1969**
1976	The Chinese Cultural Revolution
Bob Marley survives an attempt on his life.	
1980	
Political violence kills thousands.	**1986**
1988	Nuclear power disaster at Chernobyl in Ukraine
Hurricane Gilbert causes extensive loss of property and life.	
	1991
1992	Break-up of the Soviet Union
Percival James Patterson is elected the first African-Jamaican prime minister.	
1995	
The first new political party in 50 years is formed, the National Democratic Movement.	**1997**
	Hong Kong is returned to China.
2000	
Four days of violence between government officials and Kingston gangs result in the death of at least 20 people.	**2001**
	Terrorists crash planes in New York, Washington, D.C., and Pennsylvania.
	2003
	War in Iraq

GLOSSARY

ackee
A poisonous fruit with black seeds containing an edible yellow flesh.

buccaneer
A pirate of the Caribbean in the 17th century. A licensed buccaneer was called a privateer.

Creole
A hybrid language resulting from the mixing of English with the African languages spoken by slaves in Jamaica.

dreadlocks
The Rastafarian hairstyle that results from leaving the hair to naturally form locks.

ganja
Marijuana. A plant, the leaves of which are dried to prepare a range of drugs that are smoked for euphoric effect.

karst
A landscape of hills and sinkholes resulting from the erosion of limestone by rainwater. Jamaica's karst region is the Cockpit Country, where the Maroons took refuge.

kimbanda (kim-BAHN-dah)
A large drum usually covered with goat skin. It produces a bass sound and is played in *kumina* worship.

kumina (KOO-mi-nah)
A spirit religion that originates from a Congolese tradition.

kyas (kee-yahs)
A drum similar to the *kimbanda* but smaller. It produces a treble sound.

Maroons
African slaves freed by the Spanish. They lived in the inaccessible Cockpit Country and carried out guerrilla attacks on the British. Their descendants still live in central Jamaica.

mento
Music and dance descended from the slaves of Africa. The most prominent feature of the music is the regular drum beat.

ortanique
A citrus fruit hybrid cultivated by crossing an orange and a tangerine.

plantain
A greenish banana with a high starch content. It is cooked and eaten as a staple food.

Pocomania
A hybrid faith resulting from the combination of animist and Christian beliefs. The dialect name for the cult is *puckamenna*.

Rastafarianism
A Jamaican religion based partly on the Book of Revelations. Rastafarians believe in Jah Rasta, the spirit that dwells in everyone.

tam
A tam-o'-shanter, or woolen knitted cap worn by men, especially Rastafarians.

FURTHER INFORMATION

BOOKS

Baker, Christopher. *Jamaica*. 3rd Ed. Victoria, Australia: Lonely Planet Publications, 2003.

Barrow, Steve and Peter Dalton. *Reggae: 100 Essential CDs*. London, United Kingdom: Rough Guides, 1999.

Dawes, Kwame. *Wheel and Come Again: An Anthology of Reggae Poetry*. Leeds, United Kingdom: Peepal Tree Press, 1998.

Demers, John and Norma Benghiat. *The Food of Jamaica: Authentic Recipes from the Jewel of the Caribbean*. Boston, MA: Periplus Editions, 1998.

Luntta, Karl. *Jamaica Handbook*. 4th Ed. Emeryville, CA. Avalon Travel Publishing, 1999.

Mais, Roger. *Brother Man*. London, United Kingdom: Heinemann, 1974.

Pollard, Velma. *Dread Talk: The Language of Rastafari*. Rev Ed. Montreal, Canada: McGill-Queen's University Press, 2000.

Porter, Darwin and Danforth Prince. *Frommer's Jamaica*. 3rd Ed. New York, NY: John Wiley and Sons Inc., 2004.

One Love: The Very Best of Bob Marley and The Wailers. Milwaukee, WI: Hal Leonard, 2002.

WEBSITES

Central Intelligence Agency World Factbook (select Jamaica from country list).
www.cia.gov/cia/publications/factbook

CVM Television (news and entertainment station). www.cvmtv.com

Embassy of Jamaica in Washington, D.C. www.emjamusa.org

Jamaica Gleaner (newspaper). www.jamaica-gleaner.com

Jamaica Information Service. www.jis.gov.jm

The Jamaica Observer (newspaper). www.jamaicaobserver.com

Jamaicana.com (online store). www.jamaicana.com

Jamaicans.com (fun site of all things Jamaica). www.jamaicans.com

Lonely Planet World Guide: Destination Jamaica. www.lonelyplanet.com/destinations/caribbean/jamaica

Ministry of Local Government, Community Development, and Sport. www.mlgycd.gov.jm

National Environment and Planning Agency. www.nepa.gov.jm

Real Jamaican Radio 94 FM (live radio channel). www.rjr94fm.com

The Reggae Boyz (national soccer team). www.thereggaeboyz.com

The World Bank Group (type "Jamaica" in the search box). www.worldbank.org

VIDEOS AND CDS

Travels in Mexico and the Caribbean: Jamaica, Miami, and the Bahamas. VHS. Questar Inc., 1999.

Legend: The Best of Bob Marley and the Wailers. CD. Universal, 2002.

BIBLIOGRAPHY

Alleyne, Mervyn C. *Roots of Jamaican Culture*. London, United Kingdom: Pluto Press, 1990.

Baker, Christopher. *Jamaica*. 3rd Ed. Victoria, Australia: Lonely Planet Publications, 2003.

Bayer, Marcel and John Smith (translator). *Jamaica: A Guide to the People, Politics, and Culture*. New York, NY: Monthly Review Press, 1993.

Capek, Michael. *Jamaica*. Minneapolis, MN: Carolrhoda Books, 1999.

Demers, John and Norma Benghiat. *The Food of Jamaica: Authentic Recipes from the Jewel of the Caribbean*. Boston, MA: Periplus Editions, 1998.

Innerarity, Al. *Growing up in Jamaica*. Richmond, CA: BA Cross Cultural Consultants, 1990.

Levi, Darrell. *Michael Manley: The Making of a Leader*. University of Georgia Press, 1990.

Luntta, Karl. *Jamaica Handbook*. Chico, CA: Moon Publications CA, 1994.

Mason, Peter. *In Focus Jamaica*. Brooklyn, NY: Interlink Books, 2000.

Meeks, Brian. *Jamaica*. World Book Online Reference Center, 2003.

Waters, Anita M. *Race, Class, and Political Symbols: Rastafari & Reggae in Jamaican Politics*. New Brunswick, NJ: Transaction Publications, Rutgers University, 1989.

Wilson, Annie. *Essential Jamaica*. Chicago, IL: Automobile Association, 1996.

FACES: Jamaica. Peterborough, NH: Cobblestone Publications, 2001.

Land and People. Vol. 5. New York, NY: Grolier Educational Publishing Inc., 2001.

The World Almanac and Book of Facts. World Almanac Education Group, 2003.

INDEX

MAY 3 0 2007.